Economic Hierarchies, Organization and the Structure of Production

STUDIES IN PUBLIC CHOICE

Series Editor: Gordon Tullock
University of Arizona
Tucson, Arizona, USA

Other books in this series:

The intersection of economics and politics is one of the most important areas of modern social science. "Studies in Public Choice" is devoted to a particularly crucial aspect of this intersection — the use of economic methods and analysis on matters which are traditionally political in nature. Prominent scholars, such as Duncan Black, Kenneth Arrow, Mancur Olson, Vincent Ostrom, William Riker, and James Buchanan, have contributed to the development of the study of public choice. The aim of this series is to promote the growth of knowledge in this important and fascinating field.

Economic Hierarchies, Organization and the Structure of Production

Gordon Tullock

Department of Economics
University of Arizona

Kluwer Academic Publishers
Boston/Dordrecht/London

Distributors for North America:
Kluwer Academic Publishers
101 Philip Drive
Assinippi Park
Norwell, Massachusetts 02061 USA

Distributors for all other countries:
Kluwer Academic Publishers Group
Distribution Centre
Post Office Box 322
3300 AH Dordrecht, THE NETHERLANDS

Library of Congress Cataloging-in-Publication Data

Tullock, Gordon.
    Economic hierarchies, organization and the structure of
production / Gordon Tullock.
        p.   cm. — (Studies in public choice)
    Includes index.
    ISBN 0-7923-9168-3 (alk. paper)
    1. Industrial organization (Economic theory)   2. Industries, Size
of.   I. Title.   II. Series.
HD2328.T85   1991
338.6′4 — dc20   91-16453
                                                            CIP

Printed on acid-free paper.

Printed in the United States of America

CONTENTS

PREFACE

Many economists have examined the corporation, but in general they have dealt with the size of the corporation and its relationship to the rest of the society. The structure and the interior of the corporation receive much less emphasis in economic writings. It would be fair to state that most economists think if we have a system that keeps the corporations competitive and makes it possible to displace inefficient management, we will be okay.

I don't want to quarrel with this as a statement of general policy. These two criteria are important. Nevertheless, the internal function of the corporation is of interest and perhaps it can be improved, although the reader will find relatively few suggestions to that effect in this book.

In a way, I have turned away from the more general considerations that one thinks of in connection with the work of Coase, Alchain, Demsetz, Jensen, and Mechlin, and to the more detailed examination which we get in works such as those of Chandler and Drucker. Chandler is a somewhat odd person to bring in here because apparently he considers himself a historian and certainly his work has been of great historic value. On the other hand, he has great insight about the internal functioning of the organizations he studies. He doesn't produce many generalized descriptions of corporations, but he does describe individual corporations and the way things change over time. Nevertheless, his level of insight regarding the functioning corporation is significant enough to be noted by all students. The same is true of Drucker, although he does not claim to be a historian. His work, however, shows deep insight into the functioning of corporations.

The collection of economists named before Chandler or Drucker are much more conscious economic theorists. Nevertheless, they have mainly dealt with the external relations of the corporation, counting the relations between the corporations and whoever is residual claimant as part of the external relations. This is not a criticism of their work, but it is not what this book is about. My objective here is to turn attention to the interior of the corporation. The reader may think that my questions outnumber my solutions; and I won't quarrel with that. The questions are, however, important. Asking questions, frequently the first step, is as important as resolving them.

I have deviated from the current fashion of books by not providing much in the way of mathematics or notation. Although in this I follow my own personal tradition, the elimination of formal mechanism is perhaps more sizable here than usual. Organizing my thoughts into formal notation would do little or nothing to aid readers. In most cases, data are presently insufficient for actual calculating or, even when they are, the strict relationship between various variables is unknown. Therefore, many different equations could be written for the same English language proposition.

Adding these equations in might mislead by implying that the particular relationship shown by the chosen equation is the one that exists. In any event, there aren't many of them, nor are there many figures or tables. I hope this will not cause any great difficulty for the readers even though it does give the book a different appearance than most of the more modern books in these fields.

In conclusion, I should apologize briefly for one aspect of my style. I regularly tell anecdotes. One reason is that I believe it makes for easier reading. The other reason is retention: a given idea will often be retained in the reader's memory longer if attached to a mnemonic. Because this style is currently not in vogue in economics, however, my use of anecdotes has been criticized. In response, I would like to point out that the singular of *data* is *datum* or anecdote. If the reader warms up to these anecdotes, and therefore finds the book easier to read and remember, I will have achieved my objective.

In closing I should like to thank Margaret Chacon and Shirley McEwen for their assistance, as well as my research assistant Josh Gotkin, and two anonymous referees selected by the publisher who had very helpful comments.

Economic Hierarchies, Organization and the Structure of Production

1 INTRODUCTION

The first book I ever wrote — although the second book to get published — was *The Politics of Bureaucracy,* a study of large hierarchies. Although it is now partially obsolete, many of its parts have still not been fully integrated into the existing literature. This book is not a sequel, but is an effort to reconsider the whole problem from the beginning. It will deal with a number of problems that were not considered there: for example, why we have large hierarchies. There is also the problem of why so many hierarchies are small.

Indeed, if we look at most human activities, we will find a mixture of different-sized hierarchies. For instance, my house was built by a large company that builds houses all over the United States. When it needed minor repairs I hired a painter, an individual entrepreneur who normally works with one helper. Incidentally, this painter works for the large corporation as well.

Governments also have this extreme mix. Liechtenstein and the government of the Soviet Union are different-sized hierarchies, of course, and do not perform exactly the same function, but they are both governments.

If we turn to the other parts of the economy or the society, we find the

1

same kind of complicated arrangement. Family organizations vary between the extended family of some oriental societies to the tiny and rapidly shifting "family" that we see in Columbia. Church organizations range from the gigantic centralized hierarchy of the Roman Catholic Church to the usually quite small (sometimes even tiny) organizations in the evangelical Christian movement. Presumably all of them are at least reasonably efficient since they all stay in existence. Any theory of hierarchies must deal with the various sizes. It must also explain why we have hierarchies at all.

It is traditional in studies of this sort to begin with the survey of the existing literature. In this case, the existing literature is not very large if one considers theory rather than description. Descriptive accounts of various hierarchies, together usually with some general statements about how well they function or how they could be improved, are common throughout the history of social literature.

Polybius, for example, devoted some 50 pages to discussing the constitution of the Roman Republic and the military organization which was in those days the largest part of the Roman government.[1] A similar impulse to describe various government organizations and remark about their positive or negative qualities has persisted to the present day; indeed, the literature on the subject is extensive. The formal theory, however, is extremely thin in this literature as it was in Polybius's time.

Since Ronald Coase's seminal article,[2] the idea that firms in the economy exist to minimize transaction costs has been important. As far as I know, no one has formally applied that particular model to either governmental hierarchies or such things as the Roman Catholic Church, but surely the ideas behind it have wide application.

The internal structure of all hierarchies have at least some structural similarity. William Niskanen, who for many years was employed by the Department of Defense as a research economist,[3] became director of economics for the Ford Motor Company. He told me that sociologically the two organizations were almost identical.

But if the transaction model has not been much applied outside of the economic area, it has already developed difficulties there. The Yarbroughs,[4] in a very thorough survey of various points of view, list five theories that have developed out of transaction costs, although only one of them is listed as "transaction cost".

A significant characteristic of all five is that they are more accurately described as points of view, or perhaps observations, than as theory. In fact, their first category, "transaction costs," contains a number of different strains. First is the view normally credited to Williamson and his students, that highly specified forms of capital may lead to problems of exploitation that can best be avoided by vertical integration.

Although true to a considerable extent, individual enterprises also exist where this viewpoint does not seem to be important. For this reason Coase has separated himself from Williamson on this matter. Furthermore, in any event, it is hardly a general theory of organization, merely a statement that one particular condition would lead to a particular type of organization.

The Alchian-Demsetz view that organizations exist in their present corporate form largely to monitor shirking undoubtedly has much to commend it but, again, it is only a partial theory. It argues that ultimate control should be in the hands of the residual claimant but tells you little or nothing else about the organization. Both of these theories, as indeed the rest, will be discussed later in the book.

Having dealt with these transactional costs theories, the Yarbroughs turn to the "X-efficiency" literature. This is an intriguing literature in which Liebenstein has been arguing that corporations frequently are not as efficient as they could be because people do not work as hard as they could. It is interesting that at the beginning he normally recommended piece work and now recommends improvement of internal loyalty, bonding, good morals, and so on. To engage in a little long-distance psychoanalysis, I suspect the reason for the change is that in the moderate left (which is his particular milieu), *piece-rate* is a bad word, and *bonding, loyalty,* and so on, are good words. In any event, this again is not a theory of organization but is a simple statement of one aspect.

The fourth type is the "principal agent" approach in which it is usually pointed out that the principal and the agent do have at least some difference of interest; hence, control is not likely to be perfect. This is true (and certainly it was emphasized a great deal in my book, *The Politics of Bureaucracy*), but again it is not a general theory.

The next view, "the sociological", deals with group organization and the interaction of these dynamics with market forces of the firm market interface. It is not very theoretical, but anyone reading this literature can certainly learn a good deal about how corporations work in practice.

The final theory is a very abstract area, the "mechanism-design" studies which usually deal with organization in the presence of asymmetric information.

All of these things are interesting and, intriguingly, they are not inconsistent with each other although students generally regard them as mutually exclusive. All of them could be simultaneously true; all of them are largely correct. None of them, however, can be referred to as a general theory.

Admittedly, this book also will not be a general theory, but it will be much more general than any of the before-mentioned studies. It might be referred to as a general picture in which a large number of pieces of theory are integrated although the integration is not rigid enough to be referred to as one large theory.

Another difference between this study and the others we have described is that I do indeed plan to deal with all hierarchies and not confine myself to large business corporations. I want to emphasize the things that all hierarchies have in common, and I also want to deal with the many differences between the various kinds of hierarchies.

Before closing this first chapter, I want to devote a few words to eliminating a problem — not one that is difficult, but a problem that often agitates newspapers and their readers. Recently, there have been a number of drastic capital reorganizations. For a while, they were mainly takeover bids, but lately the leveraged buyout has developed. Discussion of this issue in the newspapers tends to be rather alarmist, assuming the rather odd view that buyouts involve literally eliminating parts of the economy.

Let us suppose that the management of some large conglomerate arranges a leverage buyout in which it borrows immense amounts of money in order to buy all the stock in the corporation, and then sells parts of the conglomerate in order to repay some of the loan. The view is frequently canvassed that the parts sold off will somehow cease to exist and that this immense waste of capital should instead be invested in productive equipment.

The error in the first view is obvious; the error in the second is less obvious because not everyone realizes that when you borrow a lot of money from the bank to buy something, you do indeed reduce the lendable resources of the bank you borrowed it from, but you surely increase the lendable resources of the bankers of the people from whom you buy. There should be no change in the total amount invested unless there is some systematic difference between the amount of money that is normally saved among the purchasers and the sellers.

In general, economic reorganization should be considered as something that may or may not contribute to efficiency, but does not basically change the situation of the customers, the workers (including management), and the people who put up the capital. Of course, these three groups of people overlap. The total number of people working, the total value of the capital, and the total number of customers and the amounts they put up are not greatly changed by even drastic reorganizations such as leveraged buyouts, takeover bids, mergers, bankruptcy, and so on.

Arguments exist about the efficiency of one organization or another, and there are individual winners and losers, but real resources remain unchanged. Whether the consumers are satisfied or not will depend on the efficiency of the two regimes.

To a degree, the same thing holds true when democratic governments are reorganized. The present move in England to emasculate local governments and shift their power to central government will not totally change the power of the individual English voter or civil servant, although it may well change the efficiency with which the views of the voters are implemented. Similarly, the radical decentralization of governments of both Germany and Japan imposed by the allies in 1945 did not actually reduce the government in size. It switched from a dictatorship in Germany to a democracy and, of course, that radically changed the voters' power, but a switch to a highly centralized democracy would have been just as much of a change. Thus, in general, drastic reorganizations affect efficiency but do not change the physical structure of society.

You can think of the economic hierarchies as a set of organizations in which capital holders, workers, and customers are organized to produce things that the consumers want with — we hope — minimum cost to the workers. Since workers and consumers are basically the same people, there is a question of the tradeoff between their two characteristics. A change from one organization to another can be evaluated in terms of efficiency, or aesthetic or moral characteristics, but it should be realized that these aspects all have the same goal.

Such is also the case with democratic governments and, I might even say, with dictatorships. In the dictatorship, of course, the average person does not have very much weight, but changes in the structure of the dictatorship — once again, mainly in matters of efficiency — do not change the relative importance of the dictator or common citizen. Whether the same could be carried over into religious organizations, such as the Roman Catholic Church and the evangelical churches, I do not know. All churches argue that there is a higher power favoring their particular organization. Conceivably, one of them could be right.

But this is enough of an introduction. Let us now study these various forms of organization. Because of space limitations, this book will deal briefly with various special topics attached to extensive bodies of literatures (for example, what I might call "Williamsonism") but I do not think the brevity will misrepresent these topics. Students know how to find the detailed literature. Meanwhile, let us go on with the analysis.

Notes

1. *The Rise of the Roman Empire,* Ian Scott-Kilbert, trans., London: Penguin, 1979, pp. 302–351.
2. Coase, R.J., The Nature of the Firm, *Economica,* 4 (1937), 386–405.
3. Strictly speaking, he was employed by the Institute for Defense Analyses, but since that is paid for by the Department of Defense and his work was mainly military, this is not a matter of much significance.
4. Yarbrough, Beth V. and Robert M., The Transactional Structure of the Firm — A Comparative Survey, *Journal of Economic Behavior and Organization,* (Amsterdam) 10 (1988), 128.

2 WHY HIERARCHICAL ORGANIZATIONS? WHY NOT?

The human race throughout most of its *civilized* history had one large hierarchical organization — the government; under that were several small, and mainly family, economic units in each "state". There was a powerful religious order as well, but usually it was closely integrated with the state. The situation in Europe during the Middle Ages in which the most powerful hierarchical organization was indeed the church, with the governments being a set of relatively smaller hierarchies, was unusual.

Much more common is the close connection of the state and church found in places like Hindu or Islamic principalities. Situations like ancient Sumer in which the temple was in essence the government of the city-state are also fairly common.

In general, however, over the history of man, what we think of as purely economic activities were carried on either by one big centralized organization which we can refer to as the state, the church, or the state-church, or by a large number of families working more or less on their own, although frequently with a good deal of supervision from the state. These families might be organized — normally at the behest of the state — into professional guilds, but they would carry out production in

a semihousehold way. Occasionally, there would be larger economic enterprises, but they were rare[1] and small compared to the state.

It is still true that the largest organizational hierarchies are governments, but nongovernment hierarchies of great size also exist.
McDonald's, for example, is now the world's largest private employer
with more than a million people working for it (mostly part-time). General
Motors or Exxon are also monster hierarchies that are not part of the
government. Historically there were cases of private companies which
actually were governments, too. The most conspicuous case is the Company of Merchant Adventurers to the East, with its Dutch equivalent
nearly as important. No modern corporation is as significant in the world
economy as those two organizations were in their time.

Although the traditional order was one large hierarchical organization
backed by a number of small groups, today the geni curve of organizational size would be much less deep. On the average,[2] governments are
still the largest organizations,[3] but there are very large private organizations. Why the mix?

If we look at governments alone, the problem is similar. In the first
place, there are many large, medium, and small states at any given point
in time. If we take some specific period, we will normally find some trend
for the average size to get bigger or alternatively for the average size to
get smaller, but there is no obvious long-term trend at all.

Of course, it is true that the world's population is now much larger
than it was in the days of Sumer and is more integrated by efficient trans-
portation. As a result, almost by definition the average size of the state
today is larger when measured by population. China, however, has a
smaller percentage of the world's population than it did in the reign of
Chien Lung. With respect to geographic area, the largest state that ever
existed was the Mongol Empire in the thirteenth century, and the combined Portuguese-Spanish Empire ruled by Philip II was the second largest. Both fell apart.

The twentieth century has been a period in which large states have
fallen apart and have been replaced by small states. Russia is the unique
example of a state that increased in effective size, and its gains were modest. In addition, its empire is currently disintegrating.

Thus, if we look at nation-states in the large, we find the same phenomena as in the market: that is, a wide mix of different sizes. In this case,
however, it has been characteristic of almost the entire history of mankind, whereas, as I said before, until recently the economy was organized
into two size categories: the state in its economic manifestation, and the
households.

But even this does not give adequate emphasis to the radical size differences that we see in political areas. Some believe, simply by definition, that only one government can exist in a given geographic area. Sometimes American political scientists say this, which is astonishing.

Geographic decentralization, which we call federalism, is quite common. It is not even restricted to such democracies as the United States and Switzerland. Most governments that Karl Wittfogel discussed in *Oriental Despotism*[4] granted the individual farm-villages self-government in a wide range of activities. Indeed, as a general rule, even a large city would officially be a federation of such self-governing villages (what we would call neighborhoods) taking care of many things which in Tucson (the city where I live) are the responsibility of the city government. The result is that in respect to certain minor matters, a citizen of Peking actually has more control over his government than this citizen of Tucson whose vote is diluted by votes of 200,000 others in a single unified government.

Here again is variety. The Communist Russian government, unlike the Communist Chinese government, did not permit this kind of local autonomy, although it made some sort of pretense toward doing so.[5] In democracies, France has always been notable as an area of great centralization although it has less right now than it once did. England, if anything, is increasing the degree of central control over the local government. Again, the question of why we observe these different forms of government is an open one.

Note that when we are talking about governmental structure of this sort, the citizen does not have as much control over the size of the governments to which he is subject as he does over the size of the economic hierarchies with which he deals. The individual is completely free to decide to invest his money in a fruit stand operated by one man (perhaps himself) or in stock of General Motors. He does not have the same freedom to decide the size of his government.

If we consider the individual in the market as an employee rather than as an investor, then his freedom to decide on the size of the organization he deals with is not quite as unhampered as it is for the investor, but it is still pretty free. In Tucson, I could take a job in a local restaurant or with American Airlines. In order to get an equivalent choice of governments, I would have to move.

It used to be said that the government must have a monopoly of the means of coercion. Certainly there is no such government in the United States. If I commit a crime, I might be arrested by a local policeman, state policeman, or federal policeman, depending on various details of the charge against me. All three of these levels of government institute coercion against their citizens, and the whole thing works out reasonably well.

We have here a rather astonishing difference in organization of coercion. In the United States, if you live in a city, you will have a police department where the head is an appointee of an elected government. The state and national police forces are similarly organized. If you live in the county, on the other hand, the police department is headed by a directly elected official called a sheriff, who in many cases is the most important official in the county. On the other hand, in many states both of these police forces will bring you before the same judges.

In other states the police force as a whole is fairly centralized. France is one example. France does not require anything in the way of despotic government, although the despotic government in Russia does, indeed, have a centralized police. When talking about decentralized police, I might mention Mexico, a neighbor to Tucson. They have two police forces: one deals solely with traffic and the other with all nonvehicular crimes.

It is not obvious that the state should or will control all the things we normally think of as state activities. In traditional Islamic communities, the law is not subject to legislative control by the state; it was laid down in the Koran as interpreted by an immense number of Islamic scholars. Furthermore, the judges who actually enforce the law are theologically trained and, although the local despot (and Islamic states are normally despotisms) appoints the actual judges, the selection is made from among a narrow list of people who have the necessary theological background.

The great world conqueror Tamerlane, for example, was not in any real sense master of his own household when it came to law or, for that matter, to the organization of the Islamic church in his area. Although the despots could cut people's heads off, and in fact did so, it did not mean that they could change the law as it applied to the ordinary citizens.

Nor is it even necessary that everyone in the state be controlled by the same law. The old Turkish Empire (and for that matter, a number of other countries, although the Turkish Empire had the most formal arrangement) was federalized on a nongeographical basis, that is, by religion. For the Maronite Christians, then, many of the laws that controlled their lives were those of the Maronite church. The church, in fact, maintained a small police force and had a tax system to support its governmental activities. These laws would be quite different from those imposed upon, say, the Jews by their religious organization.

Once again we find an immense variety of different organizations of various sizes and different structures. The question of why this diversity exists is important.

Throughout history most people seemed simply to have thought that this was the feature of things and did not ask any questions about it. As far as I can see, the first serious inquiry was confined to the question of why we have different kinds of economic organization, and that was asked in 1937 by Ronald Coase. He not only asked the question in his famous article "The Nature of the Firm,"[6] he gave a partial answer.[7] His originality in even asking the question should be emphasized. The article went totally unnoticed at the time, and then for many years was footnoted but apparently not read.[8]

The significant problem that Coase dealt with was probably not raised before Adam Smith wrote *The Wealth of Nations* in 1776. Before Smith, the market was thought of as simply a disorderly process, and when you thought of economic or social order, you thought of government structure or perhaps the church. Smith pointed out that the market itself is an orderly process, and most economists would argue that it is more orderly than most other organizations.

But the question that Coase posed to himself was why we have large organizations that produce automobiles, say, instead of a large number of small enterprises, each of which performs some particular operation in connection with the automobile and then bargains with other people. For example, General Motors buys the frames for its cars from A. O. Smith of Milwaukee. Its car bodies, on the other hand, are produced by a wholly owned subsidiary, Fisher Body. Why the difference? Indeed, why do we not have several tiny specialized enterprises, each performing one task on either the frame or the body under supervision of a general contractor.

Many economic enterprises have been and are decentralized; indeed, most buildings are put up this way. Monster contracting organizations may actually have comparatively few direct employees, most of them engaged in supervising the subcontractors. The garment trade in New York is another example, with large numbers of specialized enterprises that perform just one operation on a bundle of textiles and then pass it on to another organization to perform another operation.

Before Whitney revolutionized the arms industry, it was organized in this way with Birmingham, the center of the world arms trade in those days, having no large enterprises and a large number of small scale entrepreneurs who performed particular procedures. Indeed, the whole putting out system was an example of that kind of thing.

If we look at the world today, we find that there is not only a wide diversity in size of economic enterprises (we will confine ourselves to that field for the time being), but that it changes from time to time. Not long ago, there was a fad in which large conglomerates were set up to deal with different types of business under the same corporation. Special theories, in fact, were developed regarding the efficiency of this situation (to be dealt with later).

At the moment, these conglomerates are rapidly being dismantled by people who have discovered that the individual units in the conglomerate, if sold off, are worth more than the conglomerate as a whole. Clearly, this is a case in which we do not have a sound argument for any particular size of organization. Furthermore, the answer to the question of whether conglomerates are efficient in their approach to the capital market (which was earlier thought to be true) or whether the disintegration of them is efficient (which is the current fad) is by no means obvious.

We can go further here. Most American businesses started as small, closely held enterprises and only became public later in their expansion. Again, general theories were developed as to why public holdings and the stock exchange were a highly efficient method as opposed to the closed corporation with a few active managers owning all the stock. At the moment, the leveraged buyout, in which management converts a publicly held corporation into a closed company which management owns (subject to immense mortgages), is all the rage.

Note that these two changes are correlated to some extent. Some of the managements who built up big conglomerates are now organizing leveraged buyouts for the specific purpose of selling off large parts of that conglomerate and then running the smaller unit. Altogether, it would appear that we need a good deal of improvement in our understanding of the theory of hierarchies. As we proceed in this book, we will find many more puzzles as well as some fairly simple and straightforward answers.

Even if we turn to internal organization, we find a somewhat similar diversity. I mentioned before that McDonald's was now the world's largest employer. Strictly speaking, this is not true because McDonald's, although it does indeed own a large number of its hamburger stands, operates an even larger number by way of franchise. Other companies are almost entirely franchise operations; still others are almost entirely managed directly. There are also organizations like Ace hardware that operate by "reverse franchising" where the individual stores own the central organization.

There are arguments for the efficiency of all these types of arrangements, and if we look at the world in general we normally find that there is a change in one direction or the other going on: some companies will be buying up their franchises and other companies will be selling owned retail units to potential franchise operators. La Paloma, an immense and expensive resort hotel in Tucson, originally was built as a Westin franchise. Now it has been bought by Westin and is to be directly operated in the future.

This apparent lack of stable rules as to what size hierarchy is most likely to survive in business is duplicated by a similar lack of stability in government. Changes in government tend to be much slower and reverse themselves less frequently. In the United States, certainly since about 1930 for example, the central government has been slowly (some people would say *very* slowly) growing. On the other hand, France, since De Gaulle became dictator in 1958, has been moving in the other direction.

In both the United States and England efforts to move toward more decentralization have been underway but these efforts have had little effect. If we turn to centralized states, Yugoslavia, which was a centralized despotism under Tito,[9] has been disintegrating. Russia may be following the same road.

The major example of governmental shrinkage in recent years was the abandonment of their empires by France, England, Belgium,and Holland. A myth claims that these new states won their own independence by fighting. With few exceptions, this is untrue. The British army still maintains that the only colony they lost was the United States. This is not entirely correct; in some areas there was enough fighting so the British rather got tired of continuing. Malaya and Ireland, and possibly Kenya, are examples. In general, however, the independence movement was essentially British. The Congress Party of India, after all, was started by the British.

Even the nation-states in Europe are showing some slight tendencies to break up. England and France are making gestures to Scotch, Welsh and Breton nationalism. At the moment these are only gestures. Spain, of course, has a decentralized constitution, and nationalism in both the Catalonia and the Basque regions is a real phenomenon.

Most of the new countries carved out of the colonial empires have little or no reason for their present boundaries. They are simply administrative units set up for the convenience of the colonial power and have little to do with linguistic or economic coherence. So far they have largely remained intact, but the general inefficiencies of their governments are such that this may not continue. Angola was, and may be again by the time you read this, in the grips of what can either be regarded as a civil war or an invasion by a neighboring power, with the main fighting being between two linguistic groups.

In other words, we do not know what an optimal size is in any of these areas. In order to avoid disappointment, I should explain that the reader will not find a complete answer in this book. What we will discover is that a number of factors point toward larger entities and another number point toward smaller. Also, a number of factors indicate that changes, regardless of what they are, *may* cause improvements in efficiency. Factors that point toward either large or small jointly produce wide ranges in which there is little difference in efficiency, and the efficiency that is obtained shifts back and forth.

But the title of this chapter asks the question of why we see these hierarchies, and so far I have merely discussed the existence of many different kinds and sizes. We now turn to some preliminary thoughts on why they exist.

Students of ancient history have almost certainly seen the famous picture produced by Egyptian artists somewhere around 3000 BC, showing a gigantic stone block for one of the pharaoh's pyramids being towed by what looks like several hundred peasants pulling ropes; a man with a whip stands on top of the block supervising them.[10] We can all agree that this is a hierarchy, and we can also see why it existed — granted, of course, that a pharaoh had the power and desire to create the pyramid.

In this case, matters are simple. The hierarchy consists of one overseer and a large number of peasants, who, as far as we know, were conscripted for this activity. This hierarchy was, however, only part of a much larger one.

But consider the situation if a somewhat different organization had been followed. Suppose that the overseer, instead of simply ordering a labor gang, stood on his stone and offered whatever he thought was a suitable amount of money to every laborer who was willing to grab the rope and pull hard. We can even assume that instead of using a whip to encourage laggards, he simply fired them. Would this be a hierarchy? I think the answer is no, unless the particular combination of workers and overseer lasted for some time.

My definition of *hierarchy*, then, is a large number of men/women who stay together for some time, are organized into various ranks of leaders, and are led. The reader is free to use other definitions in different contexts, but if he wants to understand this book, he should remember my definition.

Suppose that the overseer had bargained with a set of small labor gangs, each of which would pull on one rope. Suppose each of these gangs had a manager and totaled ten men. Twenty such gangs are necessary to move the stone. Here is a set of small hierarchies that is each permanent but that makes contracts with various overseers to move stones.

Clearly, the small groups are hierarchies, but is there a hierarchy the whole made up of 20 of them pulling a given stone? I would say not. Provided that this grouping is purely temporary, it is a market organization. Thus, we can have small hierarchies organized for large projects by the market. The opposite is also true. When large corporations hire casual labor for specific tasks, we would have an example.

The building industry is an extreme example of market organization. Consider the situation that I, as a householder in Tucson, face in the event that I need some kind of professional assistance around my house. Since I moved in, I have hired a landscape gardener, a plumber and a painter. The painter works on his own, owns his own capital equipment, and has many different customers.[11] The plumber is part of a quite small company, and the same is true of the landscape gardener. All three of them operate in highly competitive environments, and in a real sense, so do I. I have to compete for their services by offering them prices and conditions of work that are as good as they can get elsewhere.

Note that there were only small transaction costs in dealing with these people. I asked a couple of neighbors who would be a good painter and then took their recommendation. I did not even chaffer significantly with the painter about his price or the details of his job. He had a good reputation and presumably wanted to keep it; hence, I accepted what was at that time the market price. I imagine if he had been hired by a big building conglomerate in Tucson such as Fairfield (and he does do work for them), they would have done somewhat better than I. On the other hand, Fairfield has to pay the salary of an expert to make these arrangements.

I simply selected the plumber from the Yellow Pages. The woman who answered the telephone gave me their basic price level almost immediately when I told her what I wanted. I assumed that this was the market price. Shopping around did not seem worthwhile, just as it does not seem worthwhile for me to shop around when I go to a supermarket.

The landscape architect was a somewhat more complex case because I was going to have my yard completely redone and that would cost money. I got three bids from three different landscape architecture firms. The transaction costs here were, I think, quite good because all three firms produced drawings of what they proposed to do.

All of this appears very different from the pyramid stone. The obvious difference is that literally the only technologically available means for the pharaoh to move his stone was to have it pulled by a large number of human beings or animals. He had to have them all doing the same thing at the same time. But the difference is not as great as you might think. Many highly integrated jobs require people to do either the same thing at the same time or, more commonly, to do a number of different integrated things in an appropriate time pattern, and these jobs are based on contracts with small entities.

Fairfield, a company constructing many houses in the vicinity where I live, needs to get all the work on any given house done in the right time sequence. There can be no long delays between the completion of one job and the start of another nor can there be long overlaps where the workers on one job wait for the previous job to be finished. Nevertheless, they use contracts with several small specialized contractors rather than maintaining a large hierarchical organization themselves.

Fairfield is not the only case in point. Near where I live, a new bridge is going in to replace an older one. There, too, is much skilled labor and complicated capital equipment. In any event, the capital equipment is owned by a number of enterprises which, because of the expenses involved, can hardly be called small, but certainly smaller than the contractor who is building the bridge.

Presumably, everyone who is reading this book has read Coase's "The Nature of the Firm,"[12] although many of you may not have read his more recent thoughts on the subject in the *Journal of Law and Organization*.[13] His position on the theory of the firm is frequently somewhat oversimplified into the view that the firm eliminates the costs of chaffering and bargaining between parties, that is, the transaction costs; hence, the firm is an effort to substitute hierarchical control for direct bargaining. Coase is, of course, a strong proponent of the market, as were the people under whom he studied and who originally published the article. Nevertheless, they feel that a larger organization — in many cases, skipping the market process and substituting a hierarchy — will do better.

Note that I said: "in many cases." Coase is fully aware of the existence of many other cases in which this does not work well, and I think he would agree with my contracting case as an example. With competition, particularly competition on both sides of the market (as there is in the contracting case with many contractors and many people who, say, own steam shovels and are looking for specific steam shovel-type contracts), the process of bargaining and contracting and chaffering is apt to be short and quick. The market itself will provide information as to an appropriate price and an appropriate quality.

The fact that both parties can easily switch to another agreement with someone else means that across the market relatively little attention is devoted to attempting to make specific bargains in each case which are superior to those normally found. Note that I say "relatively little". There still is some, and indeed the fact that some people are attempting to do a little bit better than the existing prices is what keep those prices in accord with shifting conditions. Many people, however, free ride on other people's surveying of prices, chaffering, bargaining, and so on.

Still, transaction costs are significant here. If the pharaoh had his stones moved by the market method I suggested earlier (in which a supervisor simply hired people one at a time for movement of one stone), there would be considerable delays while the work gangs were being put together, and these delays would be significant enough so that the work gangs themselves would develop into semipermanent institutions with only a little movement of labor from one gang to another.

The same thing develops to a considerable extent in building contracting. A number of independent contractors work mainly for Fairfield and are assigned the same supervisor. To anticipate what we will be saying later in Chapter 10 on rent seeking, however, Fairfield is a well-managed company and would see to it that these arrangements are not truthfully permanent. Too close relationships between the supervisor and the people he supervises are apt to lead to "family" arrangements under which costs may be somewhat higher and productivity somewhat lower than if the situation is always kept in a state of at least some strain.

We can make up a list of situations in which a large relatively permanent organization is best fitted for the job. One set of cases contains situations where for some technical reason — whether it is the size of the pharaoh's stone[14] or the production line first introduced on a large scale by Ford — individual bargaining with each single person at each stage is likely to evoke large costs; hence, the optimal structure is a large unit.

Even here, however, it is unclear whether these large units are necessary. Perhaps one could simply offer prices that would include as part of the contract a fine for breaking off the contract when the stone has been moved only half the distance. Contracts of this sort are rare. Mainly they are confined to actors, singers, and so on. The advantage of a large organization here is nevertheless clear.

It may be that very large organizations like General Motors or Exxon are in fact examples of this high bargaining cost situation, although they certainly do not look like it. Perhaps there are advantages in having a central control, but they are by no means obvious.

On the other hand, it is possible to have many purchasers and sellers of discrete entities, whether those entities are restaurant meals or drywall contracting for housing. The market operation would be certainly feasible and highly efficient. The strength of competition on both sides of the market makes it fairly cheap to arrange contracts; hence, transaction costs are small. Obviously, there is a continuum between these two cases.

Oliver Williamson has introduced (and others have followed his lead) the idea that under certain circumstances large organizations are relatively immune to certain types of cheating and lying. I call it "cheating" and "lying". Williamson calls it "opportunistic behavior" and "impacted information".[15] The large hierarchical organization, by bridging a particular gap, eliminates the necessity of complex contractual arrangements which would be desirable without the unified control.

This large organization, however, raises other similar problems. Nevertheless, there is considerable truth in Williamson's analysis, and there is a body of empirical evidence that his theory is a factor in establishing large hierarchical organizations in the economy.

I believe, however, that none of these theories are the basic reasons for the large hierarchies evident throughout history, which we call governments. Most governments have been despotisms of one sort or another.[16] Their leaders normally believe that one major function of the government is to get their wishes carried out. As a matter of fact, a large hierarchy is by no means perfect in this regard, as we shall see later, but it does work better than the market.

At the time the organization is set up, the despot usually does not know what his wishes will be next year. An organization that will simply obey orders, then, has its attractions. If the despot waits until next year and then offers monetary rewards for people to do what he wants, he puts himself in the situation where his bargaining power is weak, particularly if his wishes must be kept secret. Thus, a plot to assassinate a neighboring despot, for example, probably would be readily carried out by the previously existing intelligence organization, but advertising for assassins[17] would make it impossible.

Even in cases where secrecy is not necessary, the problems would be real. A despot, after all, has many things on his mind and can only devote a certain amount to each individual project. This gives him disadvantages in dealing with his own bureaucracy, but it gives him even greater disadvantages in an effort to get the market to do something it was not doing before. Thus, the decision which was made by whoever ruled Jericho in 7000 BC to build a strong wall around the city, could have, if he had relied on market procedures, put him in a distinctly difficult situation in which probably he would have faced high prices. But simply calling out the citizenry and putting them to work — which presumably is the way it was done[18] — is much simpler.

Thus, it seems that the large state hierarchies in their early days were better adapted to carrying out the wishes of the despot than a market would have been. Note that I am not criticizing the hierarchies in this case. I have no doubt that even such an oppressive government as the Assyrian was, in fact, beneficial for the average person who lived within its bounds. (Note that I say "average" Many probably would have been tortured to death while Assyria was expanding its bounds.) Roads, domestic peace, the prevention of invasions, and a regular system of taxation as opposed to arbitrary exactions are all valuable, and the Assyrians provided them just as the Romans did later.

A similar situation exists with our modern governments. A democracy is not trying to carry out the will of the despot but the rather poorly articulated will of a large number of people. Not being able to predict next year's agenda, however, except to know it will be on a large scale, means that use of the market is difficult.

In one sense, of course, all hierarchies are market organizations. They use market procedures to obtain the individuals who work for them. This, of course, only applies to those in the society who are free to make their own decisions or who, as slaves, are owned by people other than the government, but these people are always a very large part of the government, and in particular they include all the high officials of the government. The pharaoh made his pyramids with conscript labor, but his architects were not drafted.

Large private organizations may be a comparable example. Writers on corporate organization frequently refer to the Napoleon complex of the managers. Even the current tendency to have leverage buyouts of corporations would mean that individual managers — although they will be managing a smaller corporation — have much more control over it; hence, one could call that another expression of the Napoleon complex. There are, however, very strong market forces that will keep this motive in check.

Another prospect here (to be discussed in detail later) is simply that the large corporation may be more efficient in providing information for potential investors. Actually, we normally know relatively little about the corporations in which we invest, and the Securities and Exchange Commission (SEC), by making ordinary advertising illegal, probably reduces the amount of such information further.[19] Because only a relatively modest number of large corporations exist, however, the investor can more easily invest in a company that is roughly equivalent in prospect to any other large company. The market for control, first discovered by Henry Manne, is important here.

Still, smaller organizations can be effective using relatively temporary contracts, as many cases show. This chapter is titled "Why Hierarchical Organizations? Why Not?" and I cannot say I have given a definitive answer. I take considerable consolation, however, in the fact that Ronald Coase himself has also not definitively answered the question.[20]

Notes

1. Ships large enough not to be crewed by one family were needed for long voyages from quite early times. Whether experience in operating such ships was important in the organization of other enterprises, I do not know.

2. There is a significant overlap, with Liechtenstein much smaller than General Motors. As far as I know, however, in each state the government is the largest hierarchy.

3. This may not have been true in the late nineteenth century in the United States. The combination of the railroads, as the first really gigantic private enterprises, and the federal system may have led to the largest organizations being private rather than governmental.

4. Yale University Press.

5. I do not wish to exaggerate the Chinese case. There is no doubt that the village under the old empire had a good deal more control over its affairs than it does under the Communist government. Nevertheless, it is still true that local people have quite a bit of control over local matters. Wittfogel explained the system under the ancient regime as a result of declining marginal utility of administration. He argued that large hierarchies simply did not work very well in their bottom levels; hence, it was sensible to abandon the bottom levels.

6. *Economica* 4 (N.S.) (1937), 392.3

7. That Coase's answer is only partial is a fact apparently only known to a very few people, but Ronald Coase is one of them. See, for example, the R.H. Coase lectures in *Journal of Law, Economics and Organization* (Spring 1988), particularly lectures 2 and 3, pp. 19 - 47. In the final lecture he says that he is working on a complete answer to his question (pp. 46 - 47).

8. Op. cit., footnote 5.

9. He organized his despotism geographically, but the different governments of the "federated states" did as they were told.

10. There are also some fellahin putting rollers under the stone, pouring water on the road, and so on. To simplify my example, I leave them out.

11. He also has a helper for most, though not all, jobs.

12. Op. cit.

13. Op. cit.

14. Some of them were above 20 tons.

15. Actually, "impacted information" is not exactly the same as lying because a person on one side of the market may never ask the person on the other side details of his

operation. The reason he would not is because he knows he would not get a truthful answer and so "lying" is not a bad term. "Opportunistic behavior" is also not exactly cheating, although it is close enough so that creation of a new word seems unnecessary. I suspect that the use of the two new terms is simply an effort to avoid strong language.

16. See my *Autocracy*, (Boston: Kluwer, 1988).

17. The Serene Republic overcame this difficulty. Apparently in its entire history, the Council of Ten never turned down an offer to assassinate one of its enemies by free enterprisers. On the other hand, it did not get very many of them actually assassinated.

18. Of course, this was long before the invention of writing. We only know about the wall because parts of it still exist. It is also possible that the city was governed by democratic means, but if so, they still surely relied on conscription rather than the market to get the wall built.

19. SEC, of course, would claim it increases information, but as far as I know no one ever reads the brochures. Indeed, all brochures are required by law to carry in large print a false statement on the first page. This statement, which is required for SEC approval, says that the SEC has not approved the brochure. There are usually other false statements because the writers of the brochure feel that if they make accurate statements of their hopes and plans, the SEC will regard that as too strongly favorable; hence, they put in a falsely modest view. Those rare people who actually do read brochures know this and allow for it, but it is not obvious exactly how much allowance one should make.

20. See the last few pages of his third lecture in the *Journal of Law and Organization* (op. cit., pp. 46–47) mentioned before in this text. Both he and I hope to have such a solution eventually, and it is quite possible that one of the readers of this book will do so first.

3 PARALLEL PROBLEMS

Long ago when I wrote *The Politics of Bureaucracy,* I devoted considerable attention to the loss of control as orders go down or information comes up through a bureaucratic hierarchy.[1] The man supervising three people really cannot know as much as each one does about a particular problem or work unless it is very simple. He is also unable to determine how much attention each person is giving to the job. If he is supervising three people and each of them is supervising three people, the problem is compounded.

Since supervisors do not have perfect control at each stage, to some extent the people in the next stage below will be doing things which their immediate supervisors do not want, which has already deviated from the man's-at-the-top position.[2] The deviation increases exponentially as the number of levels is increased.

If we assume, unrealistically, that the individual is able to get his inferiors at each level to do 90 percent of the things he wants and that they only follow their own preferences for 10 percent, then if there are ten stages in this bureaucracy, at the bottom level only 35 percent of the output will be in accordance with the wishes of the top supervisor. On the other hand, if we have a ten-stage hierarchy with each person at each level supervising three at the next level below, we have almost 60,000 people at the bottom, and if 35 percent of their activity is that desired by the man at the top, he receives slightly more than 20,000 times as much activity of the type he desires as he would if he depended on his own labor. The attractiveness of such a hierarchy from the standpoint of the person at the top is obvious. Furthermore, as we will show later, there are a number of techniques whereby he may partially be able to outwit the exponential series.

Nevertheless, hiring 60,000 operators together with nearly 30,000 people in various supervisory roles in order to get a desired output only equivalent to 20,000 people[3] may not seem to be terribly good performance, and it could be argued that we should do our best to minimize bureaucracy forthwith. Moreover, 90 percent compliance may be too high. Table 3-1 shows the results for a number of different levels of control efficiency. The point of my next few pages, however, is to demonstrate that other forms of organization have similar difficulties of control.

We will begin with a small bureaucracy engaged in an activity that permits division of labor but which is nevertheless reasonably standardized, that is, one in which control problems should be minimal. Let us assume a small task and deal with its small problems with several different organizational structures. Say that we know of a land owner on the outskirts of Tucson who is building houses on his property. In the standard procedure, the houses at any given point in time are at different stages: while some workers are putting in the foundations on one house, other workers are putting up the structure of another, and still other houses. There is some resemblance to a production line except that the product — the house — stays still and the producing apparatus moves.

For simplicity, I shall assume that the owner hires three superintendents, each of whom hires three foremen who each supervises three laborers as shown in Figure 3-1. Napoleon thought that three was the optimal span for military matters, but there is no reason except for the sake of simplicity to believe it is optimal for our problem.

This structure per se leads to considerable labor that does not have a direct output. The three superintendents and the nine foremen are engaged in supervising rather than directly producing, and the owner is supervising them. Therefore, there are 14 people whose physical work has been dispensed with because it is thought they are more productive as supervisors than as workers. The apparatus contains 41 men, but only 27 of them are actually lifting tools.[5]

Superficially, this organization might be regarded as inefficient. Only about 70 percent of the labor force actually is doing anything on the

Table 3-1. Performance with Different Levels of Control Efficiency

Control Efficiency	95	90	85	80	75	70	65
No. of people in level 10 carrying out wishes of top level superior[a]	35335	20589	11625	6340	3325	1668	795
Percent of people in level 10 carrying out wishes of top level supervisor	59.9	34.9	19.7	10.7	5.6	2.8	1.3

NOTE: The total number of people in this organization is 88,573 of which 59,049 are at the bottom level actually engaging in activities with respect to the outer world. The remainder are supervisors of one sort or the other. The table makes no attempt to estimate how many times accident would lead to deviation from one of the lower level supervisor's desires by his inferior to have the inferior force doing what the higher level supervisor wants.

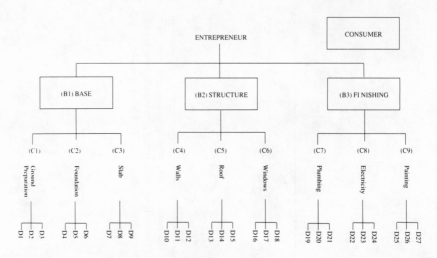

Figure 3-1.   Structure of the building industry.

houses, though the supervisors are earning their keep by organizing the work and making certain that those 70 percent work carefully and continuously. With the supervisors lifting tools instead of supervising, the total amount of useful work might be considerably less.

How should we organize this tiny structure: market, hierarchy, or some compromise between the two? Let us look at Figure 3-1. A customer off to the right is, in a real sense, the ultimate employer of these people. He will, if the enterprise is successful, buy the house; and if no customer can be found to buy the house, the whole enterprise will collapse. Moreover, the more satisfied the customer is, the higher the price is that can be charged him; hence, the more prosperous the whole affair will be.

In most circumstances today, the customer buys the completed house from the entrepreneur. Let us begin with that system and inquire into different ways in which the entrepreneur could organize his production technique. First, he could simply hire the complete hierarchy we show in Figure 3-1. For the building trade, this is quite unusual although you may have to be a little perceptive to note it. People in the trade will frequently refer to hiring someone, when, as a matter of fact, it is an independent contractor that they are dealing with even if that independent contractor is just one person.

My painter, with his single assistant, probably would tell people that I have hired him, not that I have entered into a contract with him, although there is a bid arrangement and I do not even see him while he is working. The only reason I know that he usually has an assistant is that I talked to him briefly when he was working on the house next to mine and he introduced his assistant.[6]

As the second system, the entrepreneur could hire superintendents for roles B_1, B_2, and B_3, and then actual foremen for C_1-C_9, with them contracting the work out to individual laborers. This is not a common arrangement but it is theoretically possible. In a way, employment in the building trade does tend to resemble this system because, although we do have someone who, say, owns a bulldozer and does ground preparation with the aid of a couple of assistants, he does not guarantee them permanent employment. If he does not get a contract, his assistants are normally laid off.

Another procedure would be simply to hire the B_1, B_2, and B_3 people and have them arrange contracts with C_1-C_9, who could have permanent relations with their employees within their little organization. This is essentially the way Fairfield operates. No one person is in charge of one particular house. Specialists in various activities contract the work out for several houses at a time.

Interestingly enough, these specialists are not necessarily all that competent. Most of the houses in the particular subdivision where I live have had their roofs re-tiled, courtesy of Fairfield, because the contractor who did the original tiling had not paid careful attention to the local building code. Apparently, the supervisor had missed it.

Last, but by no means least, the entrepreneur could contract out everything, that is, the B_1, B_2, and B_3 levels, or alternatively, could actually skip those levels and take on C_1, C_2, and so on. Many of the so-called intermediate-sized building projects are done this way. If, for example, you want a swimming pool you will go to someone who (after you have accepted his bid) agrees to build your swimming pool, but who will contract out a large part of it to various other entrepreneurs. Sometimes he himself does one part. Let us suppose that the entrepreneur digs the hole using his own equipment but contracts out everything else. Many other mixes of direct operation and contracting are not only possible but common.

Also, within this same structure, the entrepreneur might contract things out at the B level, and the B's would have permanent hierarchies working for them. As far as I know, this practice is not common in the building trade, but a lot of clothing — particularly hats — are made this way.

So far, we have only dealt with one possible variable because we have assumed that the customer buys the finished product from the entrepreneur who organizes his production even if he does not produce it. There is no intrinsic reason why this is necessary. It would be quite possible, for example, for the base contractor B_1 to prepare the land, sell it complete with foundation and slab to B_2, who would build the structure and sell it to the finishing contractor, who would then sell it to the customer.[7] This particular organization is not common. In Tucson, for instance, many building lots for commercial use are prepared for construction by the owner before he sells them. Indeed, one company is advertising space near my house with the slab and foundation provided.

Furthermore, the same thing could proceed with the Cs. In other words, a series of sales could transfer the property from one specialist to another, with the painter actually selling it to the final customer. Again, this procedure is not seen very often.

Outside the building trade, however, or the building trade as a whole, a large part of the ultimate object sold to the customer has actually been purchased rather than manufactured by the organization who makes the sale.

Leonard Read wrote a famous piece, "I, Pencil,"[8] in which he demonstrated that the lead pencil, composed as it is of a number of products — specialized wood, special paint, lead (which itself is a compound of several things), the rubber eraser, and the metal holder that attaches the eraser to the wooden shaft — is such that no one knows how all of these items are made. The pencil manufacturer buys most of these various things without paying much attention to how they are made, and the people who produce each material do not know too much about the others.

This situation is not abnormal. "Value added" by any given manufacturing process is characteristically a long way from 100 percent of the sale price.[9] I pointed out in connection with Table 3–1, control tends to gradually evaporate or attrit in descent through a large hierarchy. The same phenomenon will be found in purchase and sale.

First, as I pointed out, a large part of the hierarchy will not actually be doing anything other than supervising and coordinating. Similarly, if we have a purchase and sale arrangement under which, say, C_1 prepares the ground, sells to C_2, and so on, a large number of people will themselves be involved in the transactions: salesmen, purchasing agents, and so on. It is not obvious which group of "nonproductive"[10] personnel is larger. In the real world we do not see the kind of straight-line production shown here, with the project moving from C_1 straight through to C_9, but it is still true that large volumes of intermediate goods are purchased by the "manufacturer."

Not only is the chain of supervisory personnel a source of attrition but market stages are also. The first stage will rarely be exactly what the customer wanted. I recently bought one of these Fairfield mass-produced houses in Tucson. I am satisfied with it, but if I had been able to control the production, I would have designed it differently. Although we usually do not notice it, almost none of the articles that we consume in our daily life is really optimal from our standpoint.

There are several reasons for this. First, as Oliver Williamson has emphasized, if there are monopoly-monopsony relations between the purchaser and seller of some intermediate good, then the transaction cost is apt to be high. Furthermore, the probabilities that the good will not be exactly what the purchaser wants is also high since the seller has strong motives to save money and then conceal the fact that he has done so.

There are various ways of getting around this. I am on the board of directors of a small company in Iowa that has recently put a large piece of capital (large from the standpoint of the small company) into purchasing a special machine which will be used solely to produce a special product for a large company, one of our customers. We will be this product's sole source and chances are slim that we will be able to sell the product of our machine to anyone else. An elaborate contract has been drawn up to protect both parties against what Williamson refers to as "opportunistic behavior." Still, the problem is real.

Suppose that we have competition, however, as in the case of the building trades. You can buy lumber from one of many suppliers; the same is true of cement blocks, backloaders, and so on. Furthermore, local contractors engage in all stages of construction, and they are also in competition with each other. Cases of what we might call "Williamson problems" are of relatively little importance in home building, a fact of which Williamson is aware.

Another problem is that the final purchaser has little control over what goes into his/her house, swimming pool, or whatever. At each stage, the competitive market is producing things thought to be saleable not to one but to a large number of people. This has advantages, obviously, in that mass production permits lower costs. In addition, aiming at a large number of people enhances the company's reputation for producing high-quality goods.[11] Retail stores are also important in the reputation of the individual producers. Thus, the customer, in dealing with Fairfield or the retail store, depends on the reputation of the large ultimate seller and not on the reputation of the producers of the various intermediate goods.

But from the viewpoint of the ultimate purchaser, the products are (1) standardized at all stages, and (2) do not exactly fit his desires. The ultimate outcome is that we are all much wealthier than if everything were perfectly designed for our purpose and had an equivalent price. I am not complaining, but this lack of exact fit does have strong resemblance to the attrition of control that we showed in Table 3-1.

Thus, the hierarchical control and the market transmission appear to have similar defects. First, both require many nonproduction employees. In the hierarchy, they are supervisors, inspectors, and so on, and in the market, they are the sales and purchasing officials. Second, there is a loss of control. The people at the top of the hierarchy cannot depend on the people at the bottom to do exactly as they wish; in the market transmission the people purchasing the later stages of production cannot always know that the earlier stages have been done according to their wishes.

Which set of problems is most important in any given area? If we look at the real economic world, we find radical mixes of different forms of organization. For example, for a long time IBM made all of its computers from scratch. Only recently have they begun buying chips. Other computer companies have been as successful (they started smaller and still are smaller, but their rate of growth has been impressive) by buying almost everything — even contracting out final assembly. In summary, the efficiency of these various methods is not vastly different.

Figure 3-2 will seem familiar to any economist since something similar was drawn by Cantillon about 250 years ago. It shows the situation in a general form. We have a group of people who are both the producers and the consumers, and some kind of productive apparatus which I have listed as "black box". Black box is the collection of industrial and commercial organizations included with the government and churches, since I intend to cover all hierarchies, not only the markets, that convert people's property and labor of the people into items of consumption.

In the standard economic diagram, there is another set of arrows going the opposite direction which indicates the flow of money. I left them out because in many hierarchies there is no flow of money. To take one conspicuous example, after the October revolution in Russia, Lenin turned his attention to organizing a communist state. He adopted what he thought to be the efficient way: to simply abolish the market and have everyone do things as a result of direct orders from the center.

The system was a catastrophe. After a short period, Lenin announced that the failure was caused by the war. He renamed it war communism, and switched back to a modified form of capitalism called the New Eco-

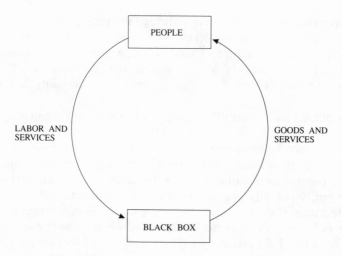

Figure 3-2.   Cycle of production.

nomic Policy (NEP). It is still true, however, that a great deal of the productive activity in communist states is the result of direct orders rather than the transmission of money. Gorbachev is trying to change this at time of this writing.

Nor is it only in the communist states. I served in the U.S. Army in World War II, and although they paid me a small sum, this pay had substantially nothing to do with my military service. I was ordered in.

As a successful example of this same system, the highly efficient cotton plantations of the Old South had slaves comprising their labor force who were not compensated in the form of money for their work. As part of the economy of the plantation, they produced most of what they themselves consumed, as well as the principle export good, cotton. In the off periods of the cotton labor demand, they built their houses, produced their food, and to some extent, their clothing.

Indeed, a certain amount of production by noncompensated producers is part of almost every economy. Governments regularly order people to do things in addition to paying taxes. Dukakis urged that instead of having a government health insurance program, private employers should provide it. Most government activity, in fact, has this characteristic. The ultimate consumers of government activity, assuming that we do not regard the employees as the sole consumers, get the services free and are then taxed.

There is no effort whatsoever to bring the taxes paid by any individual person into equality with the services and goods that he/she receives from the government. Indeed, most modern writers in this area would regard such equality as positively wicked. Redistribution is considered as one of the most important purposes of government, and certainly, is one of its major acts.

The black box in Cantillon's diagram is something we usually do not investigate. Actually, it is a box containing many smaller black boxes. Organizations take some resources, perform some particular act on them, then transfer them either to the final customer, or more commonly, to another organization within the black box that performs further steps, and so on. Eventually, the customer gets the product.

Note that this diagram is extremely general. Suppose that one of the people is Louis XIV after his famous confrontation with the Parliament of Paris. A lot of the consumption that he received was simply reports of activities of his armies somewhere in Germany. Nevertheless, he counts in our agreement both as a provider of resources (because after his famous meeting with the Parliament, he, for all intents and purposes, owned everything in France) and as a consumer. Furthermore, his direct consumption in the form of the Palace of Versailles was pretty small potatoes in terms of the total budget he allocated.

With solely economic activities, however, hierarchies are frequently engaged in different activities relatively unrelated to each other. One example of this is any large retail chain, whether it is direct or franchised. These chains do other work in addition to supervising their stores. They may provide canned goods and have warehouses, but basically they are a large collection of stores with a hierarchy above them. Individual stores do not perform services for other stores in most cases.

Many corporations are diversified in the sense that although they engage in manufacturing, they manufacture radically different things in radically different places. I am personally involved in a mild way with a small conglomerate of this sort which is in four businesses, three of which are in the same two-digit (but separate three-digit) brackets, and the other — which, interestingly enough, is the largest in terms of gross volume — is in another two-digit area. There is nothing particularly unusual about this arrangement.

Large conglomerates are frequently in the news because of their tendency either to be created by takeovers or to be disintegrated by selling off their units, whether from leverage buyout of directly. In many cases, there is substantially no connection between the various enterprises except the management. That is true of my little company if one is willing to concede our single computer as part of the management.

There are two explanations for this kind of unification other than simple historic accident.[12] First, management may be a highly skilled group whose talents would be wasted if they were confined to one division of the larger organization. It is even possible that there are economies of scale in higher management. Thus, if your company producing, say, automobiles, is not large enough to absorb the economies of scale, you will buy an electronics company and go into the satellite business as Ford did.

Second, this unification is an improvement in the capital market. The management of this conglomerate acts as an intermediate between the people who loan money and the people who buy stock, allocating the funds among its divisions in what it thinks is an efficient way. There is a certain plausibility to this argument, but the details of working it out are quite difficult.

Banks and other lenders are presumably fairly well informed about people to whom they lend the money; stockholders usually are not. Buying stock in one of the 500 conglomerates is not necessarily any more simple or more rational than buying stock in an investment trust which in turn has bought stock in, say, ten small corporations. Still, it is efficient and could have genuine information advantages. In this case, as in many of the other cases in this chapter, the outstanding conclusion one comes to is that we do not understand why different hierarchical structures exist.

Another problem is who or what should control a hierarchy. Large economic organizations, for example, may be managed by the workers, the stockholders, or possibly by a self-perpetuating board. There have been a number of famous efforts to solve this problem.[13] The whole literature has been destructively surveyed by Henry Hansmann,[14] who demonstrated that the basic argument for stockholder control is full of holes. I should also note that his proposed replacement for it (only vaguely outlined in his article) also seems full of holes.

The large publicly held American corporation whose actual structure was very heavily affected by some rules enacted by the New York Stock Exchange many years ago, is not particularly typical of world corporations. Nevertheless, if we confine ourselves to American business, we first notice the existence of a set of large, successful organizations — the mutual insurance companies — which have what amounts to a self-perpetuating board of directors.

Nominally, they are owned by their shareholders, but, in practice, the management is an in-group which selects its own successors. Because many of these corporations have lasted longer and been more successful than the standard corporation, this is a problem for the Alchien and Demsetz, and Jenson and Meckling view.

Let us now turn to governmental hierarchies. Different societies allocate different amounts of their total resources to government control as opposed to private control. They also allocate different parts of their control of resources to religious hierarchies, nonprofit organizations, and families. These will be little discussed later in this book, not because I think they are unimportant, but because I do not know much about them.

As mentioned before, the government has traditionally been the largest hierarchy in any state, the head of which is a single person. In other words, dictatorships or hereditary monarchies continue to be the normal form of government in the world. Let us begin with them and then turn to feudal and electoral systems which are historically less common.

Dictatorships or monarchies, as the case may be, are not all of the same scope. A government like the one in pre-Gorbachev Russia, which attempted total control of its subjects, is unusual. The normal dictator or monarch is interested only in the part of his subjects' lives that contribute toward his security or income.

Rulers have military forces for the purpose of preventing competitors, local or foreign, from removing them from the throne. They also have a police system that assists in collecting taxes and prevents various things like theft, which would reduce the total taxpaying ability of the subjects.

Normally, also from the very earliest days, governments built roads because they were necessary for the various organs of the government. Message systems, which evolved into the modern American post office, were established by the government, although the old Chinese Empire apparently depended extensively on private transmission of government messages from its center.

In addition, there is usually a deep connection between the government and a religion. It is not obvious whether the liaison is primarily motivated by the fact that the ruler believes in the religion or whether the connection is simply a way of firming up government control. In modern times, many dictators have not been particularly religious and in some cases have tried to disestablish religion without re-establishing another one of their own. The Marxists, of course, are simply religious crusaders who do not like competition.

Although the foregoing represent the foundations of most large governments in history, other things have been done: splendid quarters, large harems, and so on. Most rulers are altruistic enough that they also make some efforts to help the poor, improve the economy, and other such acts.

Whether they are successful in these matters depends less on their good will than on their knowledge of what would work.

This kind of government has two types of organization: a series of large functional division spread throughout the country or a series of geographic subdivisions, each of which carries out functions of government.

Readers of Herodotus will remember in the description of the Persian army that, in essence, each province of the Persian Empire sent a unit; these units were radically different from those of the other provinces. This government depended primarily on geographic distribution of power. The emperor appointed governors but did not insist on uniformity. The Jews, to take but one example, gained a great deal from this policy.[15]

A less common method is one in which the government is divided not geographically but functionally. The ruler maintains an army with garrisons everywhere. A police ministry will have offices scattered throughout; the engineering division will build roads all over, and so on. Normally, most governments have been geographic with some aspects of specialized functional division. The central government of the United States is not dictatorial, but like many other governments in federal areas, it is divided functionally rather than geographically. Of course, that is compensated by the fact that the states make up a geographic division but are not part of the federal government.

The reason for the predominance of geographical subdivisions is that it is probably easier for the central government of the dictator or king to control. It is easier to compare governors and decide who is doing the best job than it is to compare the heads of a set of different functional entities, all of whom have radically different tasks. Still, the kind of attrition of control we have discussed before occurs here.

It is interesting that in the Oriental despotisms which, after all, have controlled most of the human race during most of history, the hierarchy did not go all the way down to the bottom. Villages and, for that matter, small sections of the city, were self-governing in a more or less electoral way. Wittfogel[16] argued that this was because of the declining marginal return on administration, that is, as the administration got bigger, it was sensible just to forget about the bottom levels. These Oriental despotisms were very large and the reasoning behind Table 3–1 was particularly germane to them, though it is difficult to prove.

I have mentioned before the peculiar circumstance of Mohammedan states where the law was not under the control of the government. It should be pointed out that Mohammedan countries, which are in areas where precedents for Oriental despotism has already been established, normally do not permit local self-government by the villages.

Another intriguing example comes from one of the largest empires the world has ever known, the old Spanish Empire. The local municipalities were self-governing, but the people who engaged in the self-government, although residents of that locality were appointed by the king, or more commonly, by his viceroy. This arrangement permitted genuine decentralization without loss of central control.

Again, we observe a spectrum of different organizational structures and no particular tendency for this spectrum to change over time. With the development of more efficient communication methods so characteristic of the last 200 years, movement to the functional rather than the geographic method of control has been the dominant change. Certainly, the functional side of this mix of functional and geographic division of power is more prominent now than it used to be. This may also account for the fact that most modern governments make more effort to control larger aspects of the lives of their citizens than they used to. In theory, the old Chinese Empire was a completely monolithic organization with everyone under direct control of the emperor,[17] but in practice the villages were mostly self-governing.

Historically, another rare form of government is feudalism. Many people whose background is European think that feudalism is a standard stage in the development of society. This is simply expanding Western Europe to the world. In fact, there are only two absolutely clearcut cases of feudalism: Western Europe and Japan during the Ashikaga. Greece during the period we refer to as Mycenaean, and the Rajputs in India from roughly 1500 to the end of the British raj, could possibly be other examples.

Most of the societies that are frequently called feudal are, in fact, centralized monarchies. In some cases, centralized monarchy collapses; when it does, the individual segments do not have the loyalty to the center that would be called true feudalism, nor are they within their area dependent on feudal inferiors.

The system of feudalism provided that most of the area of the country was governed by people who had a hereditary right to do so; this hereditary structure was similar to a hierarchy. In Europe, the titles emperor, duke, viscount, and count were all ranks in the old Roman army. Thus, the king of England had under him a certain number of dukes who each had under them a large number of viscounts; counts, had under them rulers of individual manors, and so on.[18]

The degree to which they would follow orders from above was always somewhat dubious; indeed, there were legal codes as to how long the king could call out the army. It was a disorderly system and a rare one, probably explained by the fact that its lack of a formal structure made it an incompetent form of government. We therefore discuss it only briefly here.

A Knight of Great Renown[19] is a biography of the medieval European knight who was mentioned most often in written sources. The extraordinary diversity of his life is the most impressive characteristic of the book. He was the hereditary lord of Lausanne, then part of Savoy, where he was born and where he died. Most of his life, however, was spent traveling around Europe in the interest of the English king, and in the course of these duties, he also became lord of the Channel Islands.

The other form of hierarchy is one dominated at the top by some kind of electoral system. I say "some kind of electoral system" because one in which theoretically all adults can vote is only a recent development. Nevertheless, since ancient Sumer, we have had situations in which the higher officials were selected by voting, with a considerable number of people permitted to vote. This system, like feudalism, has been relatively rare — although not as rare as feudalism — which probably indicates it is not highly stable despite its popular appeal. Still, it has sometimes lasted for long periods.[20] The Roman Republic, for example, endured almost 500 years from the time the Tarquins were thrown out until Caesar seized control. Athens seems to have lasted even longer, although during at least half of its history, it was simply an administrative subdivision of the Roman Empire. Probably the longest lasting organization of this sort is Venice, which lasted almost 1,000 years from the time it was first founded (on the mainland, not in its present location) until its conquest by Napoleon.

We are not as interested in the form of the government itself as in its hierarchical structure. In case of democracies, the issue of whether to have a central government or a highly decentralized one becomes a rather different issue in the case of dictatorships. A federal system like the United States or Switzerland, in which a given voter is both a voter in and the subject of at least three levels of government, is perfectly feasible. In this case, the sub black box, which is government within Figure 3–2, itself has a series of black boxes inside it, each of which is called a government or set of governments.

If we contrast a centralized democracy like France before De Gaulle with a decentralized one like Switzerland in the nineteenth century, we see that the principal difference lies in the structure of the higher hierarchy. The centralized one has a big hierarchy, and the decentralized one has a moderate-size hierarchy for the central government and then a set of smaller hierarchies for the local governments. In the United States, during many stages of our development some individual states probably had more employees than the federal government, excluding government military forces. Even including them, it still may have been true since militias did exist in the states.

Therefore, we must consider not only how large the scope of government will be in a democracy, but whether it will be one government or many. Again, these are questions on which I have elaborated in other publications, but I have only briefly sketched here.

This chapter has certainly raised more questions than it has answered. In my next chapter, I will begin my attempt to solve them.

Notes

1. *The Politics of Bureaucracy* (Washington, D.C.: Public Affairs Press, 1965). Reprinted, University Press of America, Lanham, MD, 1987.
2. By coincidence the deviations from the desires of the lower level supervisors might lead to accidentally following the desires of the top supervisor in some cases.
3. In more exact terms, there are a total of 88,573 people in our hierarchy. Of these, 59,049 are in the bottom layer where they have contact with the outside world.
4. Coincidentally, the mistranscriptions of the orders of the supervisor in level 9 might cancel out exactly opposite similar mistranscriptions in the higher level. Thus, the number of people in the lower level doing what the ultimate superior wanted might be greater than shown. But it is equally likely that some of the 40,000 would be doing what the top man wanted if there were no hierarchy at all.
5. I have somewhat oversimplified the problem. The bottom level contractor with three employees may quite frequently spend only part of his time supervising them and part directly working.
6. My painter is an American citizen of Mexican ancestry, but very Americanized. His assistant is, I suspect, an illegal immigrant whose English is very poor.
7. The only pure case I know of where each stage of "production" is completed by an owner who then sells the product to the man who performs the next act, is the production and shipment of stone axes by some backward tribes in northern Australia. See Sharp, Lauriston. Steel Axes for Stone-Age Australians, *Human Organization* II (2) (1952), 17–22.
8. Foundation for Economic Education, Irvington on Hudson, New York, 1927.
9. I am involved in a small company in Iowa in which the value added tends to be about 20 percent of the wholesale price.
10. The Marxists actually do believe such people are nonproductive.
11. In this case, the reputation is normally not the reputation with the final purchaser, but the reputation with various intermediate purchasers. Fairfield recently discontinued the use of the type of sliding door that is on my house because it required a 2¼' screw which is hard to get even for a company as big as Fairfield. This is a minor defect in which the sliding door manufacturer has no direct contact with the ultimate customers.
12. I believe in my particular little company, and in many other cases that it is just that — historic accident.

13. See Alchien, Armen and Demsetz, Harold. Production, Information Costs, and Economic Organization, *American Economic Review* 62 (1972), 777; and Jenson, Michael and Meckling, William. Theory of the Firm: Managerial Behavior, Agency Costs, and Ownership Structure, *Journal of Financial Economics* 3 (1976), 305.

14. The Ownership of the Firm, *Journal of Law, Economics and Organization*, 4, (2), (1988), 267–303.

15. The Jews were, of course, reasonably grateful for the favor of the emperor. The Old Testament actually once contained imperial decrees in the original Persian.

16. *Oriental Despotism*, (New Haven: Yale University Press, 1954).

17. As a single example of this, if the magistrate, the emperor's representative in a given county, visited the home of someone, protocol provided that the magistrate was the host because the house, after all, really belonged to the emperor.

18. Earl was an Anglo-Saxon title, marquess is a corruption of the German margrave.

19. Esther Rowland Clifford (Chicago: University of Chicago Press, 1961).

20. So, of course, has feudalism.

4 IN THE BELLY OF THE BEAST

Having raised a number of questions in the three preceding chapters, I am now going to try solving them. I do not think I will solve them completely, but, then, neither has anyone else. My strategy might impress the reader as unusual. Instead of looking at the whole hierarchy from the outside, I will attempt to look at it from the inside. We will consider the situation of a person within a large hierarchy.

This strategy must be based on the conviction that from the inside, most large hierarchies are the same. That is, a junior official in the marketing organization of General Motors and a vice-consul in Bogota[1] really face similar situations. They must please their superiors if they want to be promoted. This involves a mixture of doing things that the superiors want done, and simply of politicking.

I mentioned earlier that William Niskanen went from a period of association with the Department of Defense into academe for a short time, and then into a corporate setting as director of economics for Ford Motor Company. He told me, "A bureaucrat from the government moving into Ford Motor Company is all set to hit the ground running." In other words, these structures are much the same.

I can add my own personal experience in this respect since I was in the Department of State for a while, was in private business as a subordinate in a law firm for a short time, and since then, as a member of the board of directors in a small company, have been at the top. To quote Niskanen again "Sociologically, they are the same."

Niskanen's rapid change is hardly contrary to the general experience of mankind. People switch back and forth from government to private enterprise quite readily in the United States, in England, and in Japan. An extreme case is when generals or admirals become heads of corporations. Usually they do quite well.

According to historical judgement, the army of the Roman Republic was the best the world ever saw. It was commanded by successful politicians. Their consuls were roughly equivalent to our presidents, and the largest forces Rome sent out were called consular armies because they were directly commanded by consuls.

One significant difference between activity in private business and in government, however, is that the objectives in private business are better defined and measured. I pointed this out in my original *The Politics of Bureaucracy*.[2] Building on that book, Anthony Downs produced a sensible terminology.[3] He suggested that we use the word *bureaucracy* for an organization whose output is not evaluated in the market. The word *bureaucrat* would be applied to any individual whose output is not evaluated in the market.

This pair of definitions means that it is possible to be a bureaucrat in a nonbureaucratic organization (for example, someone in the general counsel's office of General Motors), and to be a nonbureaucrat in a bureaucratic organization (for instance, the maintenance workers in a large government office building).[4]

The basic problem is that private enterprises in general have a fairly simple straightforward objective: to make money. Furthermore, the accounting system provides a fairly decent way of measuring the impact of various divisions of the larger enterprise on the larger enterprise's profits. Something like the general counsel's office, to a large extent, escapes this measurement process because, although the costs can be easily evaluated, the benefits are hard to put a price on.

The government agencies, on the other hand, normally do not have as simple and clearcut an objective. Moreover, whatever it is, is hard to measure. Consider the U.S. Embassy in Mexico City. The formal instructions it has received are (1) not clear, (2) partially contradictory, and (3) not always being implemented.[5]

This is not a criticism of the embassy. Formal instructions are only a small part of whatever the Department of State wants from its embassy in Mexico City. The problem is not that the embassy ignores instructions, but that its task is so big and vague that it is almost impossible to give intelligible instructions or to understand the instructions that do come their way. Furthermore, it is almost impossible to tell how well the embassy is carrying them out. The government accountants could determine the embassy costs if they tried. Actually, the accounting system used by the federal government is such that the real cost of anything is concealed. In the first place, the capital account is handled in a rather bizarre way in which basic costs are always mis-stated. Second, there is no real effort to allocate the current expenditures by function. Indeed, it is usually quite difficult to determine the exact function of embassy officials who have contact with the native country's officials.

Thus, there is a difference between working in a large corporation and in a large government office. This difference leads toward greater efficiency in the business office, which stems not from the form of organization, but from the simplicity of the objectives. Periodic efforts to improve government efficiency by assigning businessmen the task of applying "business methods" implies a simple misunderstanding of this problem. The embassy in Mexico City is not intended simply to turn a profit on its visa fees, and so on.[6] One reason we have things done by the government is that, in many cases, we do not want certain activities to be run in a profit-maximizing way.

It is an interesting fact that governments can successfully run enterprises in a profit-making way when they want. They give themselves a monopoly to make it easier. The Imperial German railway system, which before 1914 was one of the main sources of revenue for the German Empire, the Imperial Chinese postal service, which also was a major source of revenue, and the innumerable municipality-owned forests that provided revenue for many European cities or local governments of various sorts — these are all cases. A personal example I can provide is the ferry system across Lake Constance — an obscenely profitable business. Indeed, one of the arguments against building a bridge is that bridge tolls could never bring in as much as the ferry does.

Thus, in cases where the government can make cost-benefit analysis, profits may be substantial. It is likely that an employee of the Imperial Chinese postal service in, say, 1890, had a very similar set of incentives and motives as did an employee of Jardine Matheson in China during that same period. The Chinese custom service at that time was run on a comparable basis. Historically, tax-farming, which involves contracting taxes out to private businessmen, has apparently been very successful. Rome collected its taxes that way.

But aside from the advantages of having a simple objective and a method of measuring its success, corporation officials must be continually concerned with the accounting evaluation of their behavior. In other words, they must please their superiors. With a junior official in General Motors, say, the ability to please his superiors depends on his directly doing what they want much more than it does with, say, a vice-consul in Mexico City. The reason is because what the GM superiors want their junior official to do is simpler in concept and easier to measure. But if these considerations mean that private profit-making organizations will be more efficient in carrying out the objectives of the people who own them than governments will be in carrying out the rather vague objectives of the people who direct them, it does not explain the various kinds of organization that we have mentioned above. Dramatically different sizes of units and types of arrangements between diverse organizations occur in both government and private enterprise.

In both situations, politicking is important for getting ahead, although more so in a government agency such as the Department of State. I myself was not a very successful member of the Department of State[7] but the people who moved ahead fastest were specialists in dealing with their superiors. Many of them were relatively uninterested in what we might call the substantive side of the Department.

I remember one man who went in about the same time I did and rose very much faster. He had just been appointed counselor-minister of an embassy (a small one) at the time that I was contemplating resignation. He kept emphasizing the necessity of improving his bridge game because he had heard that the ambassador liked bridge. My efforts to get him to comment on the political situation (a fascinating one) in his assigned country were completely frustrated. He simply was not interested.

Although this man was typical of those who rise rapidly in the Department of State environment, he would have done badly in General Motors. Not that his concern about mastering his bridge game would have been misplaced if he had moved to a new division where the section head was a bridge fanatic; the fact that this bridge fanatic did not face an accounting test of his department's efficiency is what made the difference. In General Motors, also, if your superior is interested in bridge, it is a good idea to play it well — not enough to regularly beat him, of course. But if you do not contribute to the profit, you will go anyway. There is no profit in the Department of State.

This kind of special interest exists in many market arrangements. If you are a regular customer of an expensive restaurant, before long you will find the headwaiter addressing you by name, sitting you at a table he knows you like, suggesting the wines and dishes that will please you; the waiter may even appear with your favorite cocktail before you have ordered it. This is just like my colleague's bridge game.

What, then, is the difference between a market arrangement of this sort and the government arrangement? It is the ease of breaking contact in the market. For instance, it is not easy for me to cease being a "customer" of Pima County; it is more difficult to cease being a "customer" of the State of Arizona; and it is quite difficult to cease being a "customer" of the United States. Decisions to stop shopping at Smith's supermarket or to replace my current Oldsmobile with a car from another manufacturer are both much easier. The waiter in the expensive restaurant is aware of the fact that I can change his income quite abruptly by changing my tips,[8] but deputy sheriffs in Pima County know that I cannot easily shift to a competing supplier.[9]

Thus, in essence, the difference between a citizen's relations with a customer and his relations with his hierarchic superior is that the customer can shift to another supplier. A hierarchical superior presumably can dissolve the hierarchical relationship or impose a penalty on the individual but, in general, such a decision is more significant and requires careful thought.

My decision not to shop at Smith's would make little difference to the management, but if a number of people made the same decision, Smith's would go bankrupt. In a democracy, the same can be said with respect to the voters, but there is a subtle difference. My failure to vote for a given party literally has no effect on its future. Rarely would my vote be decisive. With regard to Smith's, however, my decision to shop somewhere else does affect them, even though very little. For them, each customer is significant, whereas in the politics of a democracy, a majority is needed.

This is merely my definition of the two types of organization, although it also fits what most people think the difference is. When I was talking about moving the pyramid stone, I emphasized the difference between a relatively permanent arrangement and a temporary one. That is also the difference in the relationships between Fairfield and its various petty contractors on the one hand and General Motors and its employees on the other. Government is impressive in this area because there a relationship is apt to be permanent, particularly in that relationship we call "citizenship".

Let us now turn to our individual who lies within the belly of the beast, that is the middle-ranking bureaucrat. A middle-level managerial employee in General Motors is presumably in a different relationship to GM than a specialized consultant called in by GM even though their incomes may be comparable. The difference is the permanence of the arrangement and the various things which that implies.

Let me look at this situation from the standpoint of Count Tolstoy.

> When Boris entered the room, Prince Andrey was listening to an old general, wearing his decorations, who was reporting something to Prince Andrey with an expression of soldierly servility on his purple face. "All right. Please wait!" he said to the general, speaking in Russian with the French accent which he used when he spoke with contempt. The moment he noticed Boris he stopped the general, who trotted imploringly after him and begged to be heard, while Prince Andrey turned to Boris with a cheerful smile and a nod of the head.
>
> Boris now clearly understood — what he had already guessed — that side by side with the system of discipline and subordination which were laid down in the Army Regulations, there existed a different and more real system — the system which compelled a tightly laced general with a purple face to wait respectfully for his turn while a mere captain like Prince Andrey chatted with a mere second lieutenant like Boris. Boris decided at once that he could be guided not by the official system but by this other unwritten system.
>
> — *War and Peace,* Part III, Chapter 9

I think anyone who has had any connection with bureaucracies will realize that Tolstoy is an excellent observer. If we wanted to represent the total structure graphically, we would need a multidimensional manifold with the points in the manifold at various levels and distances from each other; we would also need non-Euclidian geometry. To have relationships consistent, we would need many kinds of lines to indicate different types of contact. Furthermore, obviously Tolstoy is right. There are many people who are more important than their official position shows.

When I worked in an embassy in Korea, I came into contact with a number of people in the military organization. I knew one captain, for example, who occasionally had dinner with the commanding general of the 8th Army, a fact that infuriated the lieutenant-general for whom the captain was allegedly working. There was nothing the lieutenant-general could do about it, however.[10]

An individual within the bureaucracy faces a cloud of other people, some of whom clearly are more important and can affect his career; others are clearly inferiors; a very large number cannot be classified either way. If this individual wants to get ahead, he must either please his superiors or form attachments to some of them so it does not matter if he displeases others. Most large hierarchies have a sort of quasi-feudal structure in which high officials have a number of followers who do their bidding, and not that of the organization.

One particular case is the "ugly genius". This is a brilliant man who has no real prospect of getting ahead on his own because of his personality. A shrewd, smooth manipulator would regard such a person as a treasure since his only real role in life is following someone else. The genius will provide bright ideas without having the savoir-faire to double-cross his superior. I knew several pairs of geniuses and manipulators in the Department of State. If the smooth manipulator was moved to another section, within a month or so the ugly genius was transferred to the same place.

There is another type of relationship between the top and bottom of an organization: the information relationship. High-ranking officials, instead of relying solely on formal channels of information, may attach low-ranking officials with the intent of getting additional information. During the early part of his career, Kravchenko of *I Chose Freedom* was an example of such a low-ranking official. One high-ranking communist saw to it that they had an evening together once every six or seven months. Kravchenko reports the relationship in terms of awe and great privilege, which I presume it was. But I am sure that the higher official, although he enjoyed associating with a man who so obviously admired him, basically was looking for additional information on the lower levels.

Turning, then, to the Tolstoy view of how large bureaucracies work, we must begin by thinking about our middle-level bureaucrat himself rather than the organization surrounding him. Although with time this man may develop a considerable emotional connection to his organization, he is more interested in himself and his family than he is in Ford Motor Company or the Central Intelligence Agency. This may be concealed by the fact that he spends many more waking hours at Ford Motor Company or the CIA than he does with his family, but that is because he must work there in order to provide suitable family support. The company is mainly a means; his own and his family's consumption is the end.

No one thinks that the ditch digger who works hard all day to put food on the table for his family is deeply devoted to digging ditches. True, with time he will probably develop at least some rationalizations about the importance of having good ditches dug for society and the right and wrong ways of digging. This is reduction of cognitive dissonance. But he digs for his family, not for itself. The same is true for most officials in the CIA, Ford, and so on.

The higher ranks of the American government are badly paid considering their responsibilities. A certain number of these officials must be viewed as making a sacrifice to meet a public goal. This goal is not necessarily what the government wants or what the people want. It may be more particular to the individual. The fact that these higher officials tend not to stay in the jobs long is evidence that such motives are not overwhelming.

Consider an actual situation — say, the manager of Dupont's sporting powder division. The director of sales certainly will be an important person in his world as will, to a lesser degree, the assistant director, although he has no direct connection. Whether sporting powder is the largest section or the smallest in the explosive division is important to this manager. If, for example, the explosives section is larger than his, then it is likely that the head of the explosive section will probably have some power over him. Indeed, if the head of the explosive section happens to have a particularly energetic and forceful personality, he may have such power even though that division is smaller.

Officially, the contractor's bureau has no direct connection with him, but if this manager is powerful and forceful, he actually has some supervisory control over it in spite of the official organization. In other words, we are now talking about the irregular but genuine structure that we observe. In addition, our division manager undoubtedly has occasional direct contacts to both the general director of sales and the department head. Furthermore, if he is a sensible man, he has cultivated good relations with both of their secretaries.

This discussion merely sketches the complexity of actual relationships, showing that formal organization is only of general use. The individual must deal with both his superiors and inferiors. He must keep firmly in mind that there may be a Kravchenko — or several — in his immediate entourage who, although usually his inferiors, have connections with people of vastly greater rank.[11]

In addition, his closer-ranking superiors and his nominal equals will frequently have contact with his higher-ranking inferiors. Our reference official, of course, will have the same connections with some inferiors of his colleagues. Because large corporations regularly hold large-scale management meetings, even remoteness of physical location does not prevent contact between a supervisor and the inferiors of another colleague, one who may even be that supervisor's rival for a promotion.

Let us confine ourselves here to the structure of the individual's relationships with people who are not working for him — in other words, people who will influence his career other than by increasing or reducing the productivity of his division.

The first thing to be dealt with is what I call *The Grey Flannel Suit* problem. Most organizations have a rather conformist culture, not necessarily in their formal official activities but in their attitude and appearance. The grey flannel suit itself is no longer worn much by officials in corporations, but there is a certain "higher executive look" with, in general, some specialization in each corporate department.

As an example, on one occasion when I was in a restaurant in Washington, D.C., J. Edgar Hoover and one of his high-ranking assistants entered. They were both dressed inconspicuously, but interestingly their clothing was almost identical. Undoubtedly J. Edgar Hoover did not want his operatives to be readily picked out because of their clothing, but his view of inconspicuousness was clearly rather standardized.[12]

As a second example, my first assignment in the Foreign Service was in Tientsin, China. About the fifth day I was there, I was told to go down to the railroad station and pick up an incoming courier. When I asked who he was, they said they did not know and had no idea what he looked like, but that I would have no trouble picking him out. To my surprise, they were right. The fact that 90 percent of the people on the train were Chinese was helpful, but there were also about 40 Europeans or Americans. In the future, I was able to continue picking out our visitors just by clothing and manner.

As a third example, when I was in the embassy in Seoul, we occupied a small emergency building. I had a desk near the entrance. A man wearing the uniform of a colonel, but obviously not an army colonel, came in when I happened to be busy. When he stopped and looked around uncertainly, I went up and told him how to get to the ambassador, then apologized for not having given prompt attention to the local commander of CIA. He was irritated to discover that I had detected his organization. He was even more irritated when I said it was because of his uniform. I still remember him saying, "We wear the same uniform as the army."

A person who wants to get ahead in any organization should try to do things for the purpose of promotion and at the same time avoid doing things that might cause trouble. This means that in minor matters such as his clothing, he/she is apt to be conformist.[13]

One might ask why superiors act in such a way as to encourage this behavior. In some cases — for example, J. Edgar Hoover and the head of the Korean branch of the CIA — I am sure that it is quite unconscious. In other cases, it may be moderately intentional. The superior may want to give a certain impression to either his superiors or the general public.

If the supervisor does have some vague subconscious prejudices about how people should dress, he/she can evaluate the true quality of a particular inferior in matters that are important if all of the inferiors are similar along a dimension as irrelevant as clothing style. Although the reason that people tend to look somewhat alike in a given organization is their efforts to get ahead, their superior has no motive to prevent that and may, in a mild way, have a motive to promote it.[14]

Indirect connections, too, can be as important as direct ones. The individual will have social contact with people who are not very close to him/her in the organization but who can nevertheless affect his/her general reputation. My sister and her husband were low-ranking executives working for General Electric in Schenectady at one time. All of their friends were in somewhat similar positions — they held what one might call standard views that they shared. This situation was not necessarily favorable to the company. I was told by a number of them, for example, that I should avoid General Electric's small appliances because there had been too much cost engineering in them. On the other hand, what they recommended was Hotpoint, which is also owned by G.E.

A friend of my relatives was, like many of these people, engaged in auditing which was General Electric's preliminary training stage. He expressed the opinion that the auditors were attempting to be too accurate. In other words, he wanted to depend on statistics to get rid of minor errors. I do not know whether he was right or wrong about this, but the entire collection of young executives was horrified. I suspect that it ruined his career even if he was right.

Superiors are to some extent likely to pay attention to various indirect as well as direct channels of information, particularly in areas where the cost accounting system does not work. When it does work, it is easier to be accurate simply by examining it.

But, again, life is not easy for executives. The cost accounting system will permit you to compare without much difficulty, say, the 25 stores that are owned by a given chain. It may be, however, that the best and most aggressive manager is making a much lower rate of return than the manager who is the worst. The skill, talent, and hard work of an individual executive may be offset by the external environment. Accountants measure how much profit is made, they do not tell you how much is due to the external environment, the competitive pressure, and so on.

During the Great Depression, Rockford, Illinois — a machine-tool town where I was born — was badly hurt. A relative of mine had, just before the depression, purchased the Buick agency. From 1932 to 1935, no reasonably expensive cars such as Packards, Cadillacs, Lincolns, or Buicks were sold in Rockford. Buick, looking over the sales and other accounting data of their agencies, deprived him of the Rockford agency.

There is no reason to believe that the failure to sell was his fault or that there was anything he could do, considering how extremely depressed Rockford was.

In most cases today, however, the accounting system is a great boon to managers of large companies attempting to deal with their subordinates. But any manager who uses the accounting system and nothing else will be beaten by a manager who is able to use the accounting system as a guide, but then improve on it by considering the degree of competitive pressure and other factors. Even though managers of profit-seeking enterprises are in a much better situation than the managers of the Department of State in controlling their subordinates, the problems are still real.

There is also the question of how much the manager will know about one of his/her subordinates and how accurate that knowledge will be. Turn back to Table 3–1. If we think of ourselves as being a manager at the very bottom of the ten levels, it is obvious that the man at the top cannot have detailed knowledge of what each of the 58,000 people at that level is doing. Furthermore, if for some reason he did become interested in some individual and tried to use that long chain of command to get his information, the distortion would be much the same going up as going down. Therefore, with the 90-percent accuracy level in the table, about one-third of the information that he got would be accurate and about two-thirds inaccurate. Attempting to judge the efficiency of that low-level official by this method surely would be unwise, even if the higher official could spare the time to do so.

Of course, the 90-percent level is simply one we have used. I would estimate that in the case of the Department of State the 75-percent level would be more reasonable and, at that level, the "information" would be almost entirely random noise.

The lesson derived from this is not that the higher-level people can exercise no control but that the methods must in some way short-circuit the exponential deterioration in gaining information as well as in giving orders.

When I was first introduced to the Department of State as a junior officer, it was explained to me that the officials out in the field collected information that was transmitted upward, digested, and given to policy makers at the top. On this basis they made decisions which were then transferred down to us. It all seemed reasonable, but the moment you began thinking about the actual deterioration both of information and orders transferred through so many people, you realized its flaw.

Officials at the top and bottom are not merely postmen. As information goes up, it is digested and condensed, thus introducing the possibility for distortion. As orders go down, detailed implementation decisions must be made which also creates distortion. Such a simple-minded model will not work, then, and we will devote the rest of this book to methods that will work.

Let us temporarily, however, consider our individual middle-level official and his connections with the people above him. At least some of the information they receive about his actions is subject to his control. He can therefore present a better picture of his efficiency to his superiors than is actually warranted. The manager of the supermarket mentioned before is probably able to tell his superiors various things about the toughness of his competition, the difficulty of hiring labor in his area, regulations of street traffic that affect the number of people who pass by his store, and so on, without the higher officials having direct ways of finding out whether he is telling the truth.

It should be emphasized, however, that simply lying is decidedly risky. Talleyrand-Perigord, an adroit, unscrupulous man, in his activities as a diplomat, never told lies. He was very good at misleading people, but he thought that the danger of being caught in a lie, in the sense of lowering his future credibility, was greater than the advantage.[15] A superior, if you lie to him regularly, will almost certainly discover at least one of these lies and may even fire you for it.

The problem here is that the superior cannot possibly know everything about what you are doing, but he can protect his knowledge about your behavior from you. Your immediate superior has time to supervise you, and by following a quasi-random pattern of investigation, he can make it decidedly risky for you to lie to him. Misleading him without the actual words so that he believes something that is not true is also somewhat dangerous, but emphasizing the good points and hoping that no one will notice the bad points is always a fact within your control. (See Chapter 9 for further discussion.)

But the immediate transmission of information from you to your superior is not the only consideration. You certainly have rivals vying for favor who will try to find out what you are doing and pass on the bad news. This is in addition to gossip by the cloud of other people mentioned in connection with the auditors at General Electric (see Chapter 10 for more on this point).

Therefore, the individual should regard his/her superior as only partially informed about his/her behavior but as knowledgeable about aspects of it that are unpredictable. By controlling what information is passed on, the individual can influence his/her superior positively, although the degree of influence also depends on how well the superior assimilates these additional channels of information.

Note that from the standpoint of the superior, the additional channels of information are less significant for their specific content than for the fact that they provide a truth check on direct reports. The individual is unlikely to lie directly to his superior if he/she knows of this potential checking system.

It also makes sense to use your (partial) control of information to damage your rivals. The subtle but acute author of *A Practical Guide for Ambitious Politicians*[16] wrote about: ". . . the calumnies that are used to render us hated and suspected by the Prince. In calumny, two things are to be observed: the first is, is it sufficient to deprive him of the prince's favor? The second is, is it probable?" This does put the matter clearly. Of course, telling a lie about one of your colleagues in order to cause injury may hurt you if the lie is detected. It is less likely to cause you trouble, though, than telling a lie about your own work. Obviously, you might be badly informed about your colleague. Furthermore, you could perhaps put it in the form of a rumor that you have heard: "I don't believe those tales going around that Jim has been . . ."

Kravchenko, in his book *I Chose Freedom,* reported that a number of high-ranking communist officials in the days of Stalin used to deal with their colleagues by putting in their own safes "notes for my own use", indicating grounds for suspicion of a colleague. The NKVD regularly checked the officials' safes. On the other hand, since the safe owner had not made any accusations themselves, they were fairly safe if it turned out to be untrue.

Most accounts of the interior of larger hierarchical organizations deal with political maneuvering. I do not want to disparage such discussions, but it should be emphasized that actually carrying out the desires of your superiors efficiently is just as important, though nowhere near as amusing. It is difficult to generalize here, however. An official in a hierarchy will have duties, the prompt and efficient performance of which will undoubtedly move him/her upward. In different hierarchies and different times in his/her own career, these duties will vary. It is hard to write a whole book on the classic advice of "Do your job well".

In bureaucratic politicking, however, this is not so. As I have said before, sociologically all hierarchies are much alike inside. Similarly, the bureaucratic maneuvers that propelled the anonymous author of *A Practical Guide for the Ambitious Politician* ahead are also useful to someone trying to rise to the head of IBM.

The maneuvers are not as important because by way of the accounting system the higher officials in IBM have a better control than the king of France did. The fact that the king of France did not have an outstanding intellect and spent most of his time lounging with his mistresses, hunting, and so on, rather than running the country, is another reason why politicking was more important there. Still, politicking is important in both cases.

It is easy to write and interesting and lucrative best-seller like *How To Succeed in Business Without Really Trying*.[17] If Mead had written instead a detailed account of how he successfully designed advertising campaigns, it certainly would have been of interest at most to other advertisers. It probably would not have been of very much interest to them because he would have been selling different products. Sales would be limited. The book would not be amusing, although it might, in practice, be of more importance than his actual book.

In our book, we will emphasize the desirability of carrying out orders if you are a lower official. When we turn to the relation between higher officials and lower officials from the higher official's standpoint, we will discuss more thoroughly ways of getting orders carried out. Generally, the politicking, maneuvering, and so on are widespread topics, whereas the orders you receive and your actions in implementing them out are highly particular.

We are talking about a field that has had quite a bit of economics work done under the principal and agent rubric.[18] I will not elaborate on the principal-agent literature except to say that the principal cannot completely control the acts of his/her agent, and the degree of control depends on the kind of information he/she has about his his/her agent is doing. I will also not delve into the elaborate mathematics and the significant statistics that have been used in the principal-agent investigations — not because I personally disagree with them (I don't) but because I am attempting to go beyond them.

The picture can be told from the chapter title: we look at the organization from the inside, not from the outside; we consider it from the standpoint of the individual in it, sometimes an individual who is head of the organization but more commonly someone who is not. We will also confine ourselves largely to the commonalities of different types of organization.

Notes

1. The vice-consul in Bogota, since it is an embassy, would also certainly be either a second or third secretary, but I have discovered that most people misunderstand those titles. In the view of many people that I talk to, a third secretary is someone who cannot even type, and a second secretary is someone who can type but does not know shorthand.

2. Op. cit.

3. This comes from a speech I heard him give. He may have published it, but I do not know where.

4. Sometimes the bureaucracy penetrates here, too.

5. When I left the Foreign Service, the general regulations were a set of looseleaf volumes which, if my recollection is right, took up about 25 inches on a shelf. One set was kept in the administrative section of the embassy, but neither I nor anyone else of any rank in the embassy had ever read them. Their principal function was to make certain that the accounting data sent back to Washington were in proper form.

6. In the present circumstances, anyone who is permitted to sell visas would find themselves in an extremely profitable business.

7. Not because I had any objection to politicking but because I just was not very good at it.

8. Where there is division of labor, as there usually is in expensive retaurants, some of the people who serve you are not going to get any direct payment out of your tips.

9. As a matter of fact, in my contacts with them they have invariably been polite.

10. Actually, he did take the pro-forma step of exiling the captain from his normal post of duty. This meant he had more time to see his fiancee who was in Seoul working for the embassy, and, of course, had no affect at all on the frequency with which he had dinner with the commanding general. It was a foolish thing for the lieutenant-general to do and a little surprising because, although I met many stupid major-generals, and lieutenant-generals were not necessarily excellent strategists, they usually were very bright.

11. In the days when the DuPont family was actually running DuPont se Nemours, younger members of the family frequently took junior management jobs in various plants as a way of getting their careers started. It must have been rather intimidating to their formal superiors.

12. Actually, at that time lower-ranking members of the FBI were not quite so conformist, but it was still true that they were not hard to pick out.

13. In some cases "conformity" involves a deliberate pretense of "nonconformity". It may be that the person who wears an alpine hat, shall we say, scores a little bit over the one who wears a cowboy hat. A man who dresses conservatively in such an environment would be the true nonconformist.

14. In certain types of organizations, say, creative organizations like the media, there may be a myth that the really good people are nonconformists. Under these circumstances, it might be competitive to exhibit nonconformist behavior. A rigid conformist might turn up in most extraordinary clothing and engage in most extraordinary behavior simply because he is a conformist.

15. This is only true with respect to his dealings with foreign nations. He certainly misled Napoleon since, during the latter part of his career as Napoleon's foreign minister, he was also an Austro-Hungarian spy. He did not lie to the Austro-Hungarians because he knew the excellence of their information, but he also trusted their security system.

16. This book is available in a considerable number of different versions and languages, including two different translations into English. Probably the most convenient one is the one that I edited for the University of South Carolina Press (Columbia, 1961). It usually appears in indexes under my name because the author of the original is unknown. Apparently, he was an active courtier in the French monarch's court and felt that his enemies could damage him by pointing out that he was the author.

17. Shepherd Mead (New York: Simon and Schuster) 1952.

18. For reasons that may amuse the reader, this problem caused certain difficulties for me when I was, for a short period of time, in active law practice as a junior member of a firm. In those days, law libraries were not near as large as they are now; ours consisted mainly of *corpus juris* and, in fact, the first half was from one edition and the second half was from another. If you looked under agent under the "a's" it said: "See principal and agent." If you then went along to volume 38, which was in the second edition, and looked under principal and agent, it said: "See agent."

5 LIFE IN THE INTERIOR

Consider, then, the environment of a middle-level official. He/she finds himself in an organization that has many people, together with various capital items, and that has certain tasks. From his standpoint, the tasks can be divided into those that will aid him/her in getting ahead, or at least in keeping his/her present position, and those that will not. There is no ethical difference between the two categories. Indeed, when I was in the Department of State, many people were clearly carrying on agendas of their own rather than attempting to maximize the degree to which the wishes of the higher officials were carried out. These people were mostly well intentioned. They believed that what they were doing was in the best interest of the United States.[1]

But an individual aiming at objectives other than the ones of his/her superiors is, regardless of its possible moral worth, following personal preferences rather than maximizing the well-being of the organization. I call this "hobby" activity because it provides a sense of individual satisfaction. Perhaps the individual gets satisfaction by trying to do good rather than, say, embezzling funds and spending them on a lover. Although in the eyes of God these two types of deviations from orders may be radically different, both are still ignoring the commands given from on high.

The desire to do something really in accord with orders issued from superiors may lead to a serious dilemma for the low-ranking official. Suppose at the top it has been decided that the United States will press for democratic governments everywhere and always. The American ambassador in the country in which our junior official is employed, however, is convinced[2] that removing the present dictator and installing a democracy would simply be a brief way station en route to a communist dictatorship, which will be far worse for the citizens than the corrupt and rather inept dictatorship under which they now suffer.[3]

Consider a junior official in the political section of the embassy who must decide whether he should make efforts aimed at overthrowing the dictator or supporting him. Assuming the ambassador thinks that the present incumbent's overthrow will almost immediately lead to a nasty communist dictatorship, what is the junior official's appropriate course of action? Under these circumstances, he can either decide on his own which of the two policies is best and thus pursue that hobby, or he can attempt to guess as to which policy in the long run benefits him the most.[4]

For now, however, we will assume that the official's objective is to follow the course of action that maximizes his likelihood of promotion — or, at least, retention. This assumption is not arbitrary. People who maximize their career goals rise fastest; hence, they are the topmost people in a bureaucracy. Once they get to the top, however, they no longer have anywhere to go; at that point, they may change to a heavy consumption expenditure.

Our reference bureaucrat has contact with people who are his superiors, his equals, and his inferiors. Obviously, this is a rough division. There will be individuals nominally equal to him who, under certain circumstances, may be able to act as his superiors. Other people nominally his equals have special channels of information to his superiors; our bureaucrat therefore gives them careful consideration. Moreover, there will be people nominally his superiors whom he can regard as having no influence on his career or, as in the case of the general being talked to by the prince in the Tolstoy quotation, whom he can regard as his inferiors. The best way to picture this idea is as a cloud of points which we would get if we plotted the data in many statistical operations. A model plot of this kind is shown in Figure 5-1.

The individual himself is shown by the X, and the other points represent other people with their absolute vertical position indicating their rank

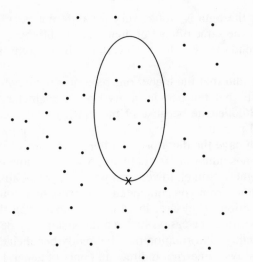

Figure 5-1.   Structure of command — The view from inside.

and their distance from him, and therefore the likelihood they have of influencing his career.

I have also drawn on this figure a rough oval representing equal amounts of power over an individual. Thus, all points within the oval are more important to him than similar points outside. We could draw a number of ovals of progressively smaller size[5] representing higher and higher levels of power. The very highest officials are not within this oval. Despite the fact that their power over him could be considerable, they are more likely not to notice his existence.

To make life more difficult, the points are continuously moving. At any given time a particular superior might be able to influence the bureaucrat's career in connection with one aspect of his work and not in connection with others. Correctly, all of this should be in a multidimensional manifold in order to show all the complexities.

Figuring out this set of relationships is a difficult problem, one that the individual must solve. There is no particular difficulty in creating a (or many) mathematical apparatus that duplicates this picture, but it is not worth the trouble. The cloud of points is different for each individual and it continuously changes. There would always be a "center of gravity", but to locate it would not necessarily be helpful.

In addition, the figures would vary for different people. Two people may be sharing the same office but their work is different enough that the shape of the cloud of points for each is radically different from that of the other.

It should be said that the higher our reference politician is in rank, the more likely it is that the people in his cloud are similar to those of an equally ranked colleague because of the roughly triangular shape of the total command pyramid.[6] If two politicians work directly under the dictator, they both have the dictator as an important part of this cloud.

I doubt that absolute rank is vital here. You may know people who are either much higher or much lower than you in terms of absolute rank but who are so remote from your immediate structure that you need not give them your attention. They are, in essence, equals even though they do not appear to be. In some cases, such a relationship may be useful to both parties. Exchange of information may be jointly beneficial even if the information is always somewhat indirect and only of general interest to the recipient. When I was in the Department of State, I had several friends in radically different branches who were, nevertheless, occasionally useful to me, and vice versa. In rare cases, we even dreamed up joint projects.

The people below you may affect your ability to get ahead. They may be information channels for people of higher rank, and this information (or disinformation) may help or injure you. More important, however, is their ability to help or injure you by their assistance in carrying out whatever project you have in mind — whether to maximize your career goals or fulfill some personal desires.

Let us apply this idea to our middle-level foreign service officer who faces various decisions regarding his activities in an embassy. He wants his junior officials to assist him whether he is trying to carry out the orders of his superiors or is trying to implement what he thinks is the ethically superior course of action (even if he is embezzling funds). He may also want to organize an apparatus of propaganda that communicates to his superior systematically biased positive data about his own activities.

This survey of the situation is intended as an introduction to this chapter which, in general, concerns people of higher rank than our reference politician. He is in the interior of the apparatus and if he is to improve or retain his position, the first people he must influence are those above him.

The simplest situation is one in which our reference politician is the direct inferior of the ultimate top man of the bureaucracy. In this case, if we turn back to Figure 5–1, there would be exactly one point in the space above him. Let us further assume that there is no prospect of our reference politician's replacing his superior. His superior is, say, the sole owner or dominant stockholder of a corporation and not a dictator since dictators are commonly replaced in their own regime by high officials.

The individual here, although close to the ultimate sovereign, is not necessarily the highest ranking official. Anyone who has read about royal courts, or the environment surrounding dictators,[7] or the internal functioning of the large corporations that have a dominant president, will know that the relative power of various individuals is different from their nominal rank. This is true even among small groups who deal directly with the ultimate sovereign.

From day to day the situation shifts and we can safely assume that our reference politician wants to be the most favored, or at least more favored. If he is the favorite, he wants to maintain that position. He also undoubtedly wants the material rewards that are in the hands of the sovereign.

Obviously, one important thing which the individual must do to a great extent is carry out the desires of the person above him. In doing so, he has some control over the information about his behavior that the superior receives about him. Furthermore, he has more expertise in his particular field than his ultimate sovereign does simply because he can devote more time to it. Thus, the individual is in a position to advise the sovereign on various courses of action.

Other people who work for the ultimate sovereign in a direct way are the individual's rivals and collaborators. Rivalry is obvious but cooperation is necessary to carry out the objectives of the sovereign. Our reference politician's attitude is a mixture of both. If there is too much rivalry, the individual's ability to control information might be jeopardized by the possibility that these intermediate subordinates will find out something negative and tell his sovereign. It is, however, foolish to believe that you can fool your superior and all your equals all of the time. In general, then, the official should do his best to carry out the wishes of his superior.

Our reference politician should also keep in mind the fact that his superior will have some channels of communication to his inferiors. Hence, information or misinformation can flow around him directly to the superior. This issue also makes it difficult for him to avoid implementing his superior's wishes. As we shall see later, however, channels of communication of this sort are not very reliable. A friend of mine, who for a short period of time was head of a large corporation, once told me that the corporation chairman must accept a certain amount of ambiguity in everything he is told.

If there are objective measures of the degree to which the individual reference politician is carrying out his instruction from on high, he should try to maximize them. In most cases they will be an approximate measure of what is wanted and not of what is actually wanted. The long and unsuccessful tussle of the Soviet government with "success indicators" illustrates the difficulty of providing objective measures of exactly what is wanted.

In the Soviet Union, the inferiors maximize the success indicator rather than concentrating on what is actually wanted. For a while automobiles were counted by their weight in determining how much a given factory had produced. When they turned to attempting[8] to penetrate the international market for automobiles, it was discovered that the Russian model of the Fiat weighed 25 percent more than it had when the plans were transferred to Russia.

This is also true with respect to accounts although the account purports to measure exactly what the people at the top are aiming at, which is the profitability. There are two problems here. First, current profitability is not necessarily a good predictor of future profitability; hence, maximizing the present discounted value of the future income stream (which is what any economist will tell you a corporation should be doing) is not perfectly measured by the accounting system.

The reason for this imperfection is the extreme difficulty of capital accounting. Accountants find it difficult to measure the net return on, say, a research effort in producing a super conducting computer as IBM once attempted to do.[9] Even if capital could be measured, it is not obvious that it would be optimal because individuals who are high officials should make estimates of the future and gamble on them. The company should pay off successful gambles and not unsuccessful ones, but the payment should not depend on any single one.

The second problem is that in large organizations, the division chiefs are doing different things. About the time that Henry Ford II relinquished active control of Ford Motor Company, the high-ranking official in charge of Ford's domestic production was producing very little profit. It would be difficult to blame him; indeed, given a few additional years of work, he began to produce large profits. The difference in profits, however, was undoubtedly due to changes in market conditions.

The problem is intensified if the different divisions are not doing the same thing. Ford was an automobile producer, and the European and American automobile factories had much in common. Ford was for a while, however, producing various components for NASA. Comparing the profitability of that business with the profitability of the automobile business and then evaluating the quality of the executives in those terms would not have been a good technique. If the NASA business was unprofitable, Ford might have wanted to get out of it. But the officials in charge might have done an even better job in difficult conditions than those officials in charge of the highly profitable Argentine manufacturing facility of Ford cars did under easier conditions.

If we move from economic enterprises to more purely political organizations such as the Executive Department of the United States or the former government of Nicaragua, the problem becomes more difficult. There are no effective success indicators here, although in a democracy like the United States, whether you win elections or lose is a somewhat similar criterion to making profits. Since the election process deals with the whole bundle of projects that the government carries out at one time, however, it is difficult to allocate that vote to any particular division.

Therefore, a comparison of the secretary of state and the attorney general in terms of who is doing the best job is nearly impossible. Even defining "a good job" is difficult. The president no doubt gives them specific orders to various areas and trusts their good judgement in other areas, but he is not really in a situation where he can do high-quality supervision. Under such circumstances, the political ability of the cabinet secretary is of greater importance than the political ability of the division chief in some profit-making enterprise. This is not because business methods are better, but simply because the object aimed at by the profit-making enterprise is somewhat easier to measure.

All this merely indicates that in a corporation the higher officials' control over junior officials is not perfect even if they are simply trying to make a profit. Their advantage is unquestioned over, say, a government official who is trying to determine whether his inferiors are efficient. Assumed, too, is the advantage that a corporate president has in dealing with staff members whose output is impossible to evaluate by accounting methods.[10] The individual in a corporation (even one very close to the top) who finds himself subject to accounting measurement will need to devote more attention to profit-making in that corporation than he would to achieving goals in a government agency. He has much less room to maneuver and to mislead his superior. Nevertheless, even in government it is safer to put effort into trying to accomplish whatever objectives your superior gives you. Political maneuvering does pay but so does genuine productivity.

Only a few people are in the distinct position of being immediately inferior to one superior. Another rare circumstance is where an individual is inferior to a group of people which acts through a voting process. In this case, these people have to be the ultimate authority themselves which means they cannot be subordinate to someone else, like Congress to the voters.

Sometimes individuals are directly subordinate to voting boards that are themselves ultimate. For example, I am on the board of directors of a company in which the directors themselves own a substantial majority of the stock. An individual in this case cannot appeal decisions to the higher authority of the stockholders. Of course, he might be able to split the board, but that is characteristic of all groups.

In a way the board has more time than an individual and, therefore, *may* have more collective knowledge, but an individual ruler would probably still be better informed. Even if the board has reasonable information, there is still considerable overlap of knowledge. Therefore, the group as a whole is not well designed to maximize its information-gathering facilities. For each individual in the group, the payoff of becoming well informed on some subject is lower than the payoff for the individual ruler. In acquiring information, each member is generating a public good for the other people. The quality of his vote is improved but not necessarily the quality of the decisions of the board.

If our reference politician were directly under such a group, he would probably receive special attention because of being an inferior. This is the most important characteristic of these groups. Attaching yourself to one or more members of the board as a kind of personal follower could be a high-paying activity. Remember that although all of them have the same number of votes, in practice some votes will be more important than others. Though it may be hard to tell which member's vote is the most important, you should try.[11]

Figure 5-1 shows a more general case in which the individual has above him many different people with varying relations among themselves as well as to him. This situation is ideal for the highly political individual because it provides maximum opportunity for maneuver; it is less than ideal for an individual who is highly productive but has few political abilities. It is unfortunate, then, that this is the normal situation. Most organizations are not small enough so that the bulk of the people are immediately under a single sovereign or group.

Before discussing this point, I want to digress briefly to say that many market activities are similar to this setup. The man running a restaurant depends on a large number of customers, some of whom are with him frequently, some of whom are not, some of whom will tell their friends that he runs a good or bad restaurant, others of whom never discuss restaurants with their friends, and so on. One could duplicate Figure 5-1 by putting his customers in the dots above him and get a similar picture. The basic difference is that in most cases there are many more dots than there would be in an organization and, partly as a result of that, the individual dots are less important to the restauranteur than they are in the hierarchical organization.

So ends our digression. To return to our situation, it is interesting that many people have written about the hierarchical organization in a rather comical vein. Sheppard Mead's *How to Get Ahead in Business Without Really Trying*,[12] The Peter Principal,[13] and Parkinson's work are examples. I presented my *The Politics of Bureaucracy*[14] to the last ambassador I worked for, now retired, who had been very successful in the Department of State. He wrote back saying he was sure that the book was intended as comedy. In fact, it was a serious book, but perhaps his reaction was influenced by the other books mentioned above.

A more detailed — and more serious — analysis can be found in my bureaucracy book and the earlier *A Practical Guide for the Ambitious Politician*[15] which I edited. Bits and pieces of relevant discussion are also scattered throughout Machiavelli, Castiglione's *Courtier,* and so on.

The basic problem here is an elderly and respectable legal topic called "principal and agent". In recent years it has attracted a lot of interest from economists. It is nearly impossible for the higher official to guarantee that his juniors will, in fact, do what he wants. Here, however, we are talking about the matter from the standpoint of the person who is below and who has his own goals. In general, the way we bring lower-level people into accord with the higher-level preferences is to take advantage of the former's own goals. They want money, prestige, and so on, which are theirs if they carry out the wishes of their superiors. Unfortunately, because of the slippage of control that we have been discussing here, the degree to which they will carry it out is always less than 100 percent.

In this situation, then, the individual should try to make careful estimates of the relative power and interest in his activities of various superiors and, if possible, arrange himself as a conduit of information to someone of high rank so that his immediate superiors are a little afraid of him. He should remember, however, that to some extent they will have knowledge of what he is actually doing. To quote an aphorism I made in *The Politics of Bureaucracy,* it does a general little good to continuously report victories if eventually he is forced to retreat through the capital city.

Thus, hard work on your immediate task is important, even if what you are doing is trivial. Chinese emperors were ceremonial figures and at various times throughout the year they went to the Temple of Heaven for services in which a designated official read pieces of the Canon. One way to get into high office in China was to impress your superiors by how you read your particular bit of the Canon. To assume the reading was a trivial matter would have been unwise.

Within most large bureaucracies there is a special circumstance that applies to both equals and inferiors: the individual could either be on or subordinate to a committee. It is important to discuss the nature of these committees before we turn to the individual and how he should behave with respect to his equals. Being subordinate to a committee is quite an unusual circumstance; usually the individual would be subordinated to one particular member of one committee rather than to the committee as a whole.

I am not talking here about a legislature or the entire voting body. These committees have been discussed in detail in other writings and rarely intrude into the bureaucracy. They act as organizations that are sovereign over the bureaucracy.

Nevertheless, if you look at any bureaucracy, private or public, you will find many committees, some permanent and some ad hoc. In general, these committees have had bad press, so we must ask ourselves why they exist if they are as inefficient as they appear.

There are a number of reasons for organizing a committee. On the governmental side, particularly in democratic governments, committees are frequently organized for the specific purpose of delaying decision on an embarrassing matter. President Reagan deferred the reform of the Social Security system until after an election by appointing a committee and telling the members to report to him later on what they thought was a good reform. This example implies that the committee essentially stalls, an easy tactic.

In the governmental process, however, committees are sometimes expected to do other things and, indeed, President Reagan's committee on reforming the Social Security system did report a number of changes that Reagan and Congress carried out.[16] Normally, however, what is wanted here is not technical advice on what a good thing to do is, but advice on what will go down well with the voters. A committee is composed of people chosen first for their prominence, not for their expertise, and second for their "representiveness," that is, they are expected to have somewhat the same reactions as the average citizen would. Committees are frequently provided with a technical staff who can deal with the details although not the main thrust of their implementation.[17]

This kind of committee has little direct effect on the career of any given bureaucrat, however, and tends to be temporary. Committees in most large organizations are both permanent and ad hoc. Again, though, they tend to have had bad press.

There are several reasons why such committees may be organized. In the government, they exist to try to minimize the bureaucratic conflicts that are such a dominant feature of Washington (and other capitals') life. If the five different government bureaus that might be involved in a particular field meet through fairly high-ranking representatives, the fighting will be taken care at that point, and any decision made by the group will then be carried out. Note that insofar as this is apt to be successful, it is necessary to find a consensus decision rather than simply to decide by majority voting.

In committees like this, an individual member dealing with people who are his equals on the committee should remember that he represents his own bureau, and his job is to maximize its well-being, not to carry out whatever the formal purpose of the committee is. He must also try to have moderately good relations with other committee members. Last, he has the problem of selling to his own bureau an outcome selected by the committee. This last task would be much easier if the outcome is to the advantage of his bureau.

If there were not higher-level people interested in accomplishing a goal, this kind of committee would never reach conclusions. Whether these people are Cabinet Secretaries, Congressmen, or the President isn't relevant; the committee is under pressure to reach some solution, and the individual bureaus represented on it realize their future can be damaged more by lack of agreement than by agreement to a solution that is moderately disadvantageous to them.

Thus, the individual on such a committee has a difficult negotiating position, but if his objective is to impress people favorably and maximize his career development, he can do so. He can also pursue some hobby to his advantage. Membership on such committees is, in general, coveted by junior bureaucrats. Senior bureaucrats normally attempt to switch the duties to junior bureaucrats because they prefer giving orders rather than negotiating.

Committees, by the way, are not always called committees. A colleague of mine who had once been a high-ranking official in a large corporation remarked that one of his corporation's better features was that they had very few committees. He then complained about how, as an executive there, he spent all his time in meetings. Cross-examination revealed that the language used in that organization labeled committees as

permanent organizations. Many temporary organizations that held meetings were not called committees. Apparently, his organization set up ad
hoc little groups whenever they confronted a problem. Their committees,
on the other hand, were permanent administrative organizations and were
quite rare.

Sometimes committees are appointed literally to seek out a solution;
they are far more common in the private sector than in government. Since
this is so, we shall concentrate here on the large corporation and their
web of special committees. The first point to be made was summarized
by Sheppard Mead, who once pointed out that the actual decision will
be made by someone who is too important to be a member of the
committee.[18]

Mead has always tended to exaggerate, but as with so many things he
has said, there is an element of truth to this remark. Normally, the results
of the committee deliberation constitute advice to higher officials rather
than an actual decision. No indication of inefficiency is implied, of course,
since turning to lower-level officials for advice is something that any sensible person will do.

Sometimes the committee will make the ultimate decision by itself, but
almost uniformly this is done by formally presenting a unanimous report
to a superior for his approval. If the matter is technically difficult and the
superior has confidence in the committee, he may approve it without giving the matter any serious consideration and, under certain circumstances, one could actually say that the committee makes the decision.
In other cases, he will regard the committee report as simply one input to
his own decision process. This process is expensive. A number of people
are convening together to discuss the matter, to study, and so on. More
people are involved than if the task were allocated to a single person.
Furthermore, the actual information transfer and study procedure is less
efficient than it is for individuals working by themselves. In other words,
if, instead of a five-man committee dealing with a given problem, you gave
to each of those five men a separate problem, the total net output would
be higher. There would be no oral communication, which is less efficient
than study; there would be no bickering for prestige among them, which
takes a good deal of energy; and there would be no attempts on individual
members to free ride on the others' information.

Delegating a task to individuals, however, brings up the problem of
supervision. People could hardly be motivated to work hard unless their
superior gave quite detailed supervision to their work. On the other hand,
the committee in a way supervises itself. Different members will keep
track of what the other members say or write, and they are apt to call the

attention of the higher officials to any default on the part of other committee members. Furthermore (and this will be discussed more fully
later), the committee winnows down the total number of ideas, a task that
the supervisor would have to do himself if he had five separate workers
dealing with the problem.

Moreover, the committee would be much less likely to engage in an
effort to replace the superior than individuals would be. This is not because the committee members are less ambitious but because the committee is a dangerous area to engage in that kind of maneuver. This
consideration is more important in the political areas of the government
than in the corporation. Indeed, electing large bodies such as Congress
and the House of Commons to vote on things, rather than electing a single
person who appears to be inefficient, does have the advantage that the
society is much safer.

The Aristotelian explanation of the overthrow of democracy starts with
the selection of a single high-ranking official to represent the people
against the oligarchy; the individual eventually subverts democracy. Although I do not want to endorse this ancient theory, many individual
examples do exist, and a single elected leader, even if the election
occurs fairly frequently, is much riskier for democracy than a legislature
is.

This idea applies to other areas as well. Kings in Europe, when they
began destroying the power of the feudal lords, turned to collegial systems under which individual ministries were headed by a board and not
by appointed officials. This move disciplined the feudal lords who sat on
these boards but who were not in the same position of power they would
have been had they been put in charge of a ministry.

The British government, which in many ways is the most structurally
conservative of modern governments, has retained all of this in the form
of the boards which are at the apex of each of their three military arms.
The admiralty, the oldest of them all, has a board called "the lords of the
admiralty." The army and the air force have boards who are not all members of the peerage.[19]

Again, this is not very important in most corporations and/or for most
governmental boards. Equal-level members of the Department of State
who meet to bicker over aid to Bolivia are not likely to subvert the state.

These boards, then, are not confined to the large corporations. Although one can argue that committees in the government — and particularly in academe — represent muddle, incoherence, and confusion, that
can hardly be true in large corporations. Most corporations are subject to
considerable competitive pressure to be efficient. Furthermore, most cor-

porations have periodic sharp downturns when they normally trim off a lot of fat.

Another pressure for efficiency in this area is the corporate raider who may decide that the corporation is so organized that, by firing the present management and hiring a new one, the value of the stock will increase enough to pay for the raid. Also, many corporations have individuals who have large enough stock holdings that they personally are very interested in efficiency.

Alfred P. Sloan, Jr., who was surely the greatest managerial genius of our epoch, owned enough stock in General Motors that the daily fluctuations of its value on the New York Stock Exchange were of greater value to him than his annual salary. Under the circumstances, he must have had an extraordinary interest in internal efficiency, particularly managerial efficiency. He was a great believer in committee government, and in his memoirs he continuously talked about his efforts to set up an appropriate structure of committees.

What, then, do these committees do? In looking through the literature, I have found little in the way of an intelligible explanation and therefore have been forced to turn back to my own ideas. In outlining a theoretical explanation, I should warn the reader that it is not a very good one, although it is as close to the truth as I can get. I urge him/her to conceive of a better one.

I also urge the reader to think about a better explanation very carefully. Almost everyone in the field pops up with an explanation of these committees, and the range of theories is wide. Most of these theories can be demolished as I consider the empirical knowledge we have about the way these committees function. Therefore, I hope that the reader does not simply accept the first thought that comes to mind as a better replacement for my solution.

In my opinion, the management of any large corporation requires a steady inflow of new ideas on various matters. These ideas are not necessarily earth-shaking. For instance, a new marketing strategy for one particular type of portable radio will not be of overwhelming importance to Sony. Nevertheless, it is important that decisions of this sort be considered, that new ideas be steadily developed, and that only the better ones be adopted. To produce quantities of new ideas is not difficult, even though most of them turn out to be inferior.

The ultimate decision on these new ideas will made be by higher-level officials.[20] But in order to economize on their time, these officials would prefer first to have the ideas generated and then sifted out by others. Not that the high-ranking officials themselves don't have ideas which frequently are better than those of their inferiors; it is just that they want a steady continuous flow and are willing to spend money to get it.

Why, then, is the committee a good vehicle? We have mentioned that individual committee members will not produce as many ideas as they would if the same individuals were dealt with separately. Assume that five junior officials produced some particular quantity of new ideas if they looked at the matter individually, and that when you subtracted the duplication there would be still a total set of, say, 25 ideas. The committee would produce fewer ideas, say, 15 — as many as three individuals operating by themselves.

They then examine this collection of ideas and rate them according to merit, passing on one to their superiors as their principal recommendation with possibly several alternatives. They are fully prepared to switch to another if the superior does not approve of it. The winnowing process will not be perfect; however, it is likely that the top idea passed on to the superior is, say, one of the three best out of our 15.

The committee, then, combines a process of generating ideas with a process of winnowing. It does neither with perfect efficiency but performs the combined task better than any other system. It particularly eliminates genuinely poor ideas early in the process so as not to waste time on them.

Careful attention should be given to the opportunity the structure provides for the strategically maneuvering and rather unscrupulous junior officials. The committee is not a good area for him/her to operate because his/her actions will be promptly noticed by rivals. He/she may, of course, be an expert in committee manipulation and may operate very well in committee; hence his/her promotion is promotion for merit. A committee, by guaranteeing much publicity for almost anything that is done, makes the more devious types of political maneuvering by officials less likely to pay off.

This, then, is my explanation of why we see all these committees in profit-making corporations, even those subject to considerable pressure. Normally, committee structure is cut back when the organization is in trouble, but that may simply indicate that they are taking relatively short-range approaches to economy rather than long-range. A company on the verge of bankruptcy is hard-pressed to make money immediately and may be willing to give up some potential for future money-making.

These remarks about the committee, however, are only a specialization of some more general remarks about the nature of corporate headquarters. Anyone who has had contact with them will be impressed with not only the number of committees there, but the number of people, many of whom do not have highly specified jobs. Indeed, the professional management advice teams that go around the world spend much of their time bemoaning this fact and suggesting that the jobs be sharply defined and that people stop getting outside of their formal jurisdiction. In spite of all this advice, the phenomenon continues.

It seems to me this whole thing — committees and this large collection of offices with various not-too-well specified duties — is a procedure for generating ideas and then winnowing them as they work their way toward the top. There are many bright people who are heavily motivated to produce profit-making ideas. They work in an environment where most of the other bright people do not really like their colleagues' ideas because they fear the colleagues will be promoted above them, but who are nevertheless interested in increasing the profitability of the corporation. Thus, the other executives will be somewhat prejudiced against any bureaucrat's ideas but not totally unwilling to consider them. The consequence is the joint production of new ideas and winnowing.

The system does not function in a way that, in the eyes of God, would be regarded as perfectly efficient; in practice, however, it would be difficult to improve. The bureaucratic swamp acts as a filter selecting the better (not necessarily the best) ideas for the higher-ups. The fact that these structures regularly and consistently escape the formal specification of job jurisdictions, thereby leaving opportunities for management advisors to tell them they should reform, is evidence that the system is more efficient with this kind of jungle.

One final item to discuss concerns an individual and his/her relation to superiors and equals. By no means are all officials convinced that they are going to advance rapidly. Therefore, many try to buy insurance to protect them in their present job. Even those who plan on moving ahead rapidly would like to have some protection on the flanks. The result is the formation of little alliances among different officials of the "you don't tell on me and I won't tell on you" form. I will discuss this thoroughly in Chapter 10, but obviously such organizations do not contribute to efficiency from the standpoint of the corporation as a whole but do benefit the people involved. Well-functioning corporations should try to minimize the formation of alliances.

The picture so far is realistic and coincides with the interiors of most large bureaucratic hierarchies, though it emphasizes disproportionately the need to engage in bureaucratic maneuvering. In any moderately well-functioning organization, an individual who wants to rise or to maintain his/her position is under considerable pressure to expend time and energy into carrying out the desires of his/her superiors. Societal or personal views are not relevant here; the objectives of the higher organization are. The best advice is: work hard at whatever you are supposed to do and also work hard at politicking. The former is likely to take up more of your time.

Notes

1. Or, in some cases, the best interest of the Koreans, the Chinese, or whatever country we were in. American diplomacy is very frequently aimed at benefitting countries other than the United States.

2. Whether correctly or incorrectly makes no difference for this example.

3. The removal of Chiang Kai-shek by civil war in 1948, the removal of Batista to be replaced by Castro and the removal of Samoza and the replacement by the communist government there, in all three cases were greatly aided by an arms embargo imposed by the U.S. on the noncommunist side.

4. General Eisenhower was sent to England by General Marshall for the specific purpose of talking the English out of the North African invasion. He ended up as its commander and, of course, this was the foundation of his later brilliant career. The intriguing feature of all of this, and evidence as to what a brilliant politician Eisenhower was, is the fact that he did not make Marshall angry.

5. It is not clear that oval is the correct shape. It would depend on the individual structure. The oval I have drawn goes through the position of the individual, but it would be possible to draw one that passes below him to indicate that even his nominal inferiors have at least some effect on him.

6. In Figure 5-1 the reference politician is far enough down in the pyramid so that its outer boundaries are of little interest to him.

7. Accounts of Tito's personal relations with his immediate inferiors when he was living on the island of Vis behind the protection of the British navy during World War II are particularly clear on this kind of maneuvering.

8. They attempt to do so about every 15 years.

9. This was before the discovery of the so-called high-temperature super conductors. It is possible that IBM will now revive the project.

10. Legal counsel and research are two areas where it is easy to measure the costs but very difficult (sometimes even impossible) to measure the benefit.

11. When Martin was chairman of the Federal Reserve Board, he was never on the losing side on any vote. A number of people thought this indicated he was extremely influential, but the chairman votes last. It is just as easy to explain this phenomenon on the grounds that he was easily influenced.

12. Sheppard Mead (New York: Simon & Schuster, 1952). Incidentally, the title is a bad misnomer. The person who follows his advice will have to try very hard. It is just that what he is trying to do is not to improve the profitability of the company.

13. Laurence J. Peter and Raymond Hull, (New York: William Morrow, 1969).

14. *The Politics of Bureaucracy,* Op. cit.

15. Columbia, SC: University of South Carolina Press, 1961.

16. As an amusing aspect, the democratic members of this non-partisan committee

refused to discuss any proposal that might injure the older pensioners until after the election.

17. In recent years, economists acting as staff members of such committees or simply as civil servants have had considerable effect on American government policy. Apparently their arguments, although not very persuasive when offered by way of TV to the general public, have considerable effect when offered in private to people who are well above average in intelligence.

18. *Op. cit.*

19. Not all the lords of the admiralty are actually members of the peerage, although in the long run they tend to be.

20. I was intrigued in reading Iaccoca's memoirs to discover that the styling committee, the ultimate decision maker on such things as the color of Ford, is actually composed of the five highest ranking officials of the company, including the treasurer.

6 STRUCTURAL REFORM

The last two chapters considered the situation of the individual official inside a hierarchy in connection with his dealings with superiors and equals. Now we discuss his dealings with inferiors. In other words, we assume that he is in a position to have other people work for him within this larger hierarchy.

Juniors will behave toward this official in the same way that he behaves toward his superiors. Furthermore, his behavior toward juniors will be as respectful as his own superior's behavior has been toward him. Just as his superiors will have developed informal contact with some of his inferiors to provide themselves with a better check over his behavior, he will form informal contacts with people several stages down the line from himself to buy similar insurance and control over his immediate inferiors.

We already know that the amount of control he will have over his inferiors is imperfect, just as the control his superiors have over him is imperfect. Let us, however, temporarily consider what he would like his inferiors to do if he had perfect control, possibly through a special divine dispensation.

First, he wants his inferiors to carry out any orders he gives them. But clearly this is only a preliminary approximation. His inferiors will know much more about their jobs and will therefore have to make many detailed decisions without his input or knowledge. Nevertheless, he wants individual lower-ranking officials to make the same decisions he would make in a similar position but with his own interests strongly at heart.[1]

Furthermore, he wants the officials to have these decisions coordinated with those made by the other lower officials. In essence, he wants a collection of robots, each behaving in accord with the higher superior's best interests and each fully informed of the others' jobs. Obviously, this is not feasible.

The individual must settle for less, then, as all large organizations do. Specifically, he must realize that his orders will be distorted as they work their way down the pattern of control. They will also be supplemented by the decisions of lower-level people who know more details about the entire area he is dealing with.

He will, of course, have the problem of obtaining information from below, and here again he must accept a certain amount of ambiguity. The generation of new ideas discussed previously is important, and he must assure that his inferiors do so even if he proposes to seize the credit himself.

This chapter will propose various structural modifications that the individual can make in the organization. Although these changes may help somewhat, they do not solve the problem totally. In other subsequent sections of the book we will discuss ways to moderate demands on his inferiors and thereby elicit better performance from them than if he attempted to implement the robot model described above.

In this discussion, we will think of ourselves as one individual trying to control his inferiors, although in a larger hierarchy things are rarely that simple. Nevertheless, knowledge of the difficulties in this simple structure will be useful in considering the organization of a larger structure. The reader may want to think of our individual as a dictator, or as the whole body of voters of the United States as a superior over our governmental hierarchy. In practice, most people who face these problems are fairly low in the hierarchy and have to worry about interference by superiors or equals. This latter aspect will be set aside until later.

We propose first to change the span of control. Table 3–1 showed how the control of a superior tends to attrit by descending organization levels and by the wonders of compound interest; thus, ten steps down, his control was limited. Suppose, however, that instead of having a span of control of three, we have one of ten. Under these circumstances, he can have ten immediate inferiors, each of whom has ten immediate inferiors; he will then have 100,000 people working for him at the bottom level with only five steps down. Thus, with any given level of distortion, the wide span of control would provide a more accurate implementation of his desires at the lower level.

The problem here is that little phrase "with any given level of distortion". Surely, as the span of control grows wider, his ability to supervise each of his inferiors shrinks, and the ability of each of his inferiors to supervise their inferiors shrinks. Therefore, the degree to which he has control shrinks. Table 6-1 illustrates this phenomenon. I have assumed that each of the rates of attrition in Table 3-1 is associated with a span of control with the 5 percent rate of attrition associated with the span of control of two, the 10 percent with three, and so forth. This table then shows for each of these pairs, the number of steps necessary to get down to a number of junior bottom officials at least roughly similar to the bottom level in Table 3-1. The table also shows the number of people at the bottom level under these circumstances, and the number of them who are actually carrying out the desires of the man at the top.

The reader will note that my interaction of the two variables, the degree of deterioration of command and the span of control, is completely arbitrary. We only know that the attrition would be a positive function of the size of the span of control. This table is intended to clarify thought rather than provide any actual result. What we observe from it is that for any particular type of activity there must be an optimal span of control. The easier it is to see what our subordinates are doing or the easier to give them instruction, the wider the optimal span of control. Thus, we observe that large corporations normally have a wide span of control over individual sales organizations. A division manager may have 15 to 20 substantially identical stores under his control. On the other hand, within the staff where it is hard to tell what the lower-ranking people should be doing and whether they are indeed doing anything, we normally observe narrow spans of control.

Each different task, then, presumably has its optimal span of control, and it is a duty of higher executives to see that their inferiors are organized that way. In this connection, the wider the span of control, the lower the number of executives needed. We cannot tell, however, what that optimum is for any given agency. Still, attempting to get an optimal span of control is important for any person trying to control subordinates.

Let us turn to other structural problems. The first one often used, but in a misleading way, is what I call the "criss-cross" form of organization, though it is commonly referred to as "staff and line." In Figure 6–1, I return to Fairfield and look at it from the standpoint of corporate headquarters. Actually, in order to present this figure correctly, I would have

Table 6-1. Command with Different Spans of Control.

Span of Control Compliance	2 .95	3 .90	4 .85	5 .80	6 .75	7 .70	8 .65	9 .60	10 .55
No. of levels	16	10	8	7	6	6	5	5	5
No. in bottom level ≈ 58,000	65536	59049	65536	78125	46656	117649*	32768	59049	1000000
Total no. carrying out head's intent	60891	32699	25297	21844	10675	17389	4706	5634	6150
Total percent carrying out head's intent	46.5	37.9	29	22.4	19.1	12.7	12.6	8.5	5.5
Total employees	131070	88752	87380	97655	55986	137256	37448	66429	111110
No. in bottom level doing head's intent	28884	20589	17858	16384	8304	13841	3802	4592	5033
No. of bottom level complying $a^L \times$ no. in level	44	34.9	27.2	21.0	17.8	11.8	11.6	7.8	5.0

Notes: a = percent of compliance.

L = no. in level.

*The figure of 117,649 doesn't seem very close to 58,000, but the use of five stages would provide an equal error in the other direction; 58,000 happens to be about halfway between fifth and sixth powers of seven.

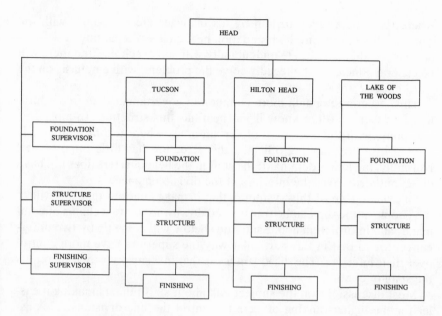

Figure 6-1. Fairfield, Inc.

to use very large sheets of paper, so the reader should regard this as only a sketch of the higher levels.

First under Fairfield is a set of divisions that builds and sells houses. For the sake of simplicity, I have put in only three such divisions. Their heads are in charge of house building in a particular city.

In addition, there is a set of staff offices in charge of various aspects of building. Once again, I have given only three: foundation, which includes ground preparation and slab; structure, which includes walls, roof, and so on; and finish, which includes plumbing, electricity, painting, and the like. Each staff officer has a connection with the person in each division who is in charge of that particular activity. Thus, the foundation man in Tucson reports to his superior who is the Tucson manager, but he is also, in a way, under the control of the foundation man at corporate headquarters.

The reason I call this a criss-cross organization is rather obvious: there are two chains of command crossing each other. Furthermore, in all the cases with which I am familiar, there is some doubt as to exactly how these two chains influence any given subordinate. The foundation man in Tucson, for example, will no doubt occasionally find himself in a situation where the orders given to him by his manager are in conflict with the general guidelines from the foundation headquarters regarding how foundations should be built. He undoubtedly will make a choice and there will be general policies that allegedly solve the problem, with emphasis on the word *allegedly*.[2]

This structure is much more common in government than in corporations. In fact, I do not know if Fairfield has this structure. In most corporations, with the exception of certain areas where technical advice is needed by lower-ranking officials, this structure has little importance.[3] Normally, the line is dominant; the staff in the headquarters does not have direct authority over the inferiors of the division managers.

One advantage of this system is that it makes certain that the will of the people at the top can be transmitted downward by two chains of command, and information about activities below will come up by two different routes so that in this particular way the superiors have more control over their inferiors. The disadvantage is that in a sneaky way it increases the span of control.

Most discussions on the subject talk about staff officers making it easier for the higher-ranking officers to control the line divisions. This assumes that the staff units do not require any control themselves, which is absurd. In the particular organization shown in Figure 6-1, the span of control for the man at the top is six: three divisions and three staff offices. The head will have less control over each of the six heads there than he would have over each of the three if he only had the line.

This structure, then, is only useful if there is doubt about the far-down inferiors carrying out orders. There are, however, a few cases in which the two channels actually simplify the total command structure. One obvious case is a corporation that deals with a single union and has a single personnel office with control spread throughout the various divisions. When dealing with a single union, a uniform policy is sensible.

Other cases have purely technical aspects. I assume that General Motors has a headquarters division concerned with engine design, which offers technical advice for engines built by many operating divisions. Such a setup is likely to be regarded by the division managers not as a hazard but a help.[4] Even here, however, confusion could be introduced if an engine designer's views of what a proper car engine is differs from the views of the man in charge of that particular line.

But, again, pure staff activities of the criss-crossing type are not common in the private sector. Even the large staff of large corporations are mainly concentrated in the headquarters or in a few regional offices and they mainly deal with each other rather than having direct connections to functional areas in the lower-ranking organizations. The staff and line criss-cross is more common in military organizations and, to a lesser extent, in other governmental organizations.

Even in the military, it was a late nineteenth-century development to provide a large number of high-ranking positions. The U.S. Army, Navy, and Air Force are all examples of many reins and not much horse. But there are more positions for generals and admirals in the reins than there are in the horse.

This structure is not often found in organizations under pressure for efficiency, but a modification of it is widespread. Let me begin with the best government bureaucracy that has ever existed, the old Imperial Chinese civil service. Its members were selected by extremely difficult examinations. The people who excelled in these examinations (people at the very top) were made censors rather than being sent into administrative positions.

The Imperial censorate consisted of a number of officials who originally were very junior although they could be promoted within the censorship ranks. They were sent on roving commissions to all of the major government units. The censor arrived at a provincial government without any formal duties except to watch the other officials. He would be younger with no previous connections with the higher officials. Censors had but one duty: to catch the officials out. If they were able to demonstrate that the lower officials were disobeying the Imperial will, their future was assured. On the other hand, bringing false charges was dangerous because they would be punished by the same punishment that the official whom they charged would have received if the charge had been true.[5]

Note that this system did not expand the span of control very much. The emperor had direct dealings in the capital with the censorate higher officials and had to devote a certain amount of attention to them. But basically he could continue dealing with the regular officials and almost ignore the censorate except when he received messages telling him that various line officials were misbehaving.[6]

This is a pure case of criss-cross line of control. It was not a line of command because the emperor did not give any commands by way of the censorate. In addition to the formal reports that went up through the regular channels, there were always intelligent, bright, and ambitious young men who were watching carefully and who had the right to raise any criticism they thought desirable. There is no doubt that this was a considerable improvement in the efficiency of the system.

Most modern corporations have something similar in the form of auditors. This is shown in Figure 6-2 which, with some relabeling, could just as well be a diagram of the old Imperial Chinese civil service.

Note that the auditors are not even the employees of the company in a permanent sense. Many large corporations do indeed have their own auditing staff for dealing with junior officials, but well-organized large corporations also contract with outside accounting firms for the highest-level audit. Furthermore, it is considered good practice to change these outside auditors from time to time. The corporation for which I serve as director does this every five years. But to repeat what has been an underlying theme of this book, the system exists only because of the fact that the corporation is attempting to make money. If it had more complicated objectives, this simple management tool would not exist.[7]

Moreover, to repeat another theme, although this management tool exists, it is not safe to depend on it completely. Nevertheless, auditing definitely improves the control of people at the top just as the imperial censors improved the control of the emperor.

Other similar mechanisms can be widely used. If some aspect of the work is routine, someone can be put in charge to see that the routine is carried out without the need to devote much time to supervision. The

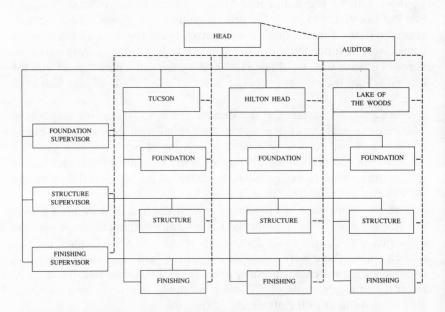

Figure 6-2.   Fairfield—The role of the auditor.

Foreign Service in which I once worked had a set of inspectors who were simply ordinary foreign service officers assigned to that job. As far as I know, they were not carefully selected and, in fact, tended to go back to the regular line after a tour of duty in the inspectorate.

Their existence had nothing to do with the higher-level problems of diplomacy. They did make sure, however, that the lower-level functions were uniform. Are the individual foreign service officers good at entertaining? Is the expenditure control in the embassy such that embezzlement is difficult? Do they keep their codes safe? Because they dealt with these types of questions, their existence undoubtedly made life easier for the higher officials.

Maybe this point can be expanded. During World War II, there was one lieutenant-colonel attached to Eisenhower's headquarters whose only duty was to travel around Europe calling on intelligence agencies to check if they were keeping their credentials (which permitted them to use a full battalion of infantry) carefully protected. This obviously required some supervision, otherwise he could have simply gone to Paris. But the amount of supervision was slight. It may be, then, that a number of simple tasks can be allocated to people who are good at routine and for which supervision is quite easy and limited.

A special category of this type is the chief of staff, a job that has developed out of military activities but is also found elsewhere more commonly in governmental areas than in a profit-making enterprise. In this case, many routine activities are put in the hands of one chief of staff, leaving the man at the top more time to deal with the policy issues. Even so, the senior still must supervise the chief of staff to some extent.

Two other cases look similar but are not the same. For one, despots who have various interests other than directly ruling — the harem, for example — frequently have a prime minister as the only official that they supervise. No doubt this means the government is one step further down the hierarchy and the ruler's control over it is less than it would be if he did not use this shortcut. On the other hand, he does have more time for his harem.

Another similar case involves a high official who acts as a lightning rod for the commander. The commander of a naval vessel is a center for loyalty among the crew, and the blame for various nasty things that happen to them, like enforcing inconvenient regulations, falls on the executive officer. This does not mean the executive officer need not be carefully supervised, but it does mean that the morale of the crew is better than if the captain himself enforced various inconvenient regulations.

The reader might have noticed that these structural possible reforms may be worthwhile, but they still do not solve the basic problems. It is still true that the degree of control shrinks as one goes down the pyramid. There are a few other techniques which, by changing the structure, may lead to the same kind of minor improvement: giving up attempts to get complete control, and aiming for a more limited goal. These methods are also useful when one's goals are more modest.

In the next example, we separate into two categories the orders which are given to junior people: (1) continuing orders (things we want them to do all the time or when some particular contingency arises) and (2) orders for specific problems that arise. In other words, the former can be regarded as general regulations although the latter are decidedly specific orders.

It is easier to get people to understand a set of orders if the same order is left unchanged for some time. Furthermore, it is somewhat easier to find out whether they are obeying because you can take a random sample over time. For example, you might inquire on 1 percent of the days if an office has filed a report that is supposed to be filed daily.[8]

This method no doubt does improve the degree to which the higher officials can control their subordinates, but again, we must not exaggerate its effect. They still must communicate their ideas to their subordinates and see that their subordinates are carrying out the permanent orders as well as the temporary ones. The effect is efficient, insofar as it is, because there are standing orders. To this extent, the higher officials can get better control by this method. Furthermore, the fact that they can economize on the amount of time spent supervising means they also have more control over the rest of the structure. But again, the span of control problem is not totally solved here. The leader must devote some time to giving the standing orders and supervising their implementation, and that detracts from the number of people they can have under their control for directly carrying out changing policy orders.

My own experience indicates that higher officials have difficulty adjusting these two different activities. Frequently, the fact that something is put into the regulations does not necessarily mean it will be kept a long time. It may only emphasize an order that will have effect only temporarily. Furthermore, as a rough rule of thumb, no one takes the obsolete orders out of the books. Thus, you have immense collections of paper in which only some pages are actually "live."

In a way, then, this system carries with it its own inefficiency. If the higher officials devoted adequate time to continuously changing the standing orders so that they are always in accordance with the desires of the superiors and the current situation, it would be very time consuming. On the other hand, if they do not (which is generally the course followed), it means that these standing orders provide much freedom for the lower officials who will decide which ones they will carry out.[9]

Although standing regulations are useful, they do not totally solve the problem of control. A couple of other organizational structures can help somewhat. These involve designing the structure in a way that pressure is put on intermediate management to carry out the wishes of the higher management, and then the intermediate management is assumed to be capable of putting the same kind of pressure on their inferiors. Obviously, such procedure will solve the span of control problem only if the intermediate managers are easier to control than the straightforward control we have described above, and there are ways of checking to see that it happens like that.

We have talked about accounting as a way of controlling lower levels of a corporation because the corporation's goal is simply to make money. Sometimes similar simple incentive structures exist for governmental units or even for parts of the corporation whose output is hard to measure monetarily. For example, for every legal dispute, the corporate counsel could be asked to give an estimate of the outcome and a recommendation for out-of-court settlement. If there are many cases, statistical determination of his/her judgement is possible. If he/she is a good attorney, the court procedures should tend to average out cases that the corporation wins and loses at about the level at which the recommendation for out-of-court settlement is justified.

But note, this system requires that there be some control on the corporation counsel since by providing poor legal performance in the court case, he/she can always lower the number of victories, and hence justify a generous recommendation for settlement. Usually this problem is solved by having outside attorneys handle the cases. Since there is a functioning market for attorneys, it is not difficult to get an idea of their quality by some method other than asking your corporation counsel.

But obviously this is an approximate, not an exact, method. As another example, consider the body count in Vietnam. The reports got negative reactions partly because the army did it badly and partly because most of the people who opposed the war in Vietnam did not like to think of killing.[10]

But the emotional objection aside, the army did fail to take any significant precautions to make the counts accurate and, indeed, apparently hoped that they would be exaggerated. Nevertheless, a combination of the body count and the resources expended by our side, battle by battle, would have made it possible to get an idea of the quality of junior officers commanding those battles. Obviously, again, you need to have a considerable number of such battles to judge any given officer. But that was no great problem in Vietnam because minor actions were almost continuous.

In both of these cases the numerical measure is not as good as the measure obtained by accounts in the ordinary corporation. We must remember also that the accounting measure is far from perfect, but we must attempt it nonetheless.

We should warn against efforts to generalize along these lines, however. The failure by the Russians to develop suitable success indicators for their economy is merely one example. In general, any government bureau can, if it wants (and it rarely does), save money easily by simply ceasing its operations.

The police department that saves money by discontinuing all patrols would not be functioning efficiently.[11] If the number of people working is not reasonably close to what is wanted, inefficiency will probably result. You will be counting something, and your subordinates will maximize whatever you are counting. If that is not close to what you actually want, this is, in essence, giving them a set of instructions which tells them to do something different from what you want.

During the Korean War, our psychological warfare branch, among its other idiocies, decided that it would deliver one billion propaganda leaflets to North Korea by air in one year. As the end of the year drew nearer, the physical size of the propaganda leaflet shrank. Toward the end, their leaflets were the size of postage stamps. Clearly, this kind of propaganda was not what the person who specified the original number had in mind.

Anyone familiar with the history of bureaucracy can find many more examples. Senior bureaucrats have too much sense to use this method when it will lead to hopeless distortion, but it is still employed sometimes when it should not be, and contrarily, sometimes not used when it should be. It is a highly specialized technique that should only be used in highly specialized circumstances but that may, in fact, improve higher-level control.

The second method of trying to pressure lower-level officials to pressure people below them, without too much span of control structure, consists of dividing the job into a number of divisions that basically do the same thing. This makes comparison easy. Thus, almost all governments throughout history have been organized geographically rather than functionally. A Roman governor in one province had tasks somewhat similar to those of a Roman governor in any other province. The comparison of the output was relatively simple, although there could still be difficulties.

In China, the Hsien magistrate was usually the only central government employee in a given county that he ran, being chief engineer, chief tax collector, chief of police, and judge. The central government paid attention mainly to two things,[12] his tax collections and the occurrence of any riots or public expressions of discontent. If he fell behind on tax collections or if there was any public rioting (perhaps about taxes), he was removed. The system was simple and reasonably functional.

This approach made it difficult for the government to get anything else that it wanted done. They used a very wide span of control roughly ten to one but the fact that they had these Hsien magistrates as the lowest-ranking, formal, central governmental officials and that these magistrates were subject to considerable pressure along at least two measurable dimensions meant that the central government would largely ignore other local matters. In other words, there were only about 2,000[13] Hsien in China, and direct government control terminated with them rather than the 300 million individual Chinese. The system worked because these 2,000 officials were occupying similar positions, making comparison easy.

Another reason it worked was the simplicity of the orders given. Each Hsien was given almost exactly the same orders as the others.[14] In a way, the span of control program had been finessed but not completely. Furthermore, as I have emphasized, it depended heavily on the state's being willing to control the local communities only along a few dimensions.

In this chapter we have been discussing ways in which the span of control, shrinkage of control going down the hierarchy, can be dealt with, on the assumption that you are going to attempt to get perfect control. I presume that the reader is aware of the fact that we have not solved the problem, although almost all our techniques can make control easier. It is important, then, that the higher-ups realize that they do not and cannot have complete control at the lower level. A perfectly integrated, perfectly functioning bureaucracy is a myth; one should simply try to make things work as well as possible. In the next few chapters we will deal with the problem of controlling an obviously imperfect bureaucracy.

Notes

1. Ed Zajac, who used to be a high official of AT&T, always told new employees that they were to try to do what the chairman of the board would have done had he known as much physics as they.

2. Any reader who is interested in how bad bureaucratic prose can get should look into the discussions in military regulations as to the relationship of, say, a division G2 to

the division commander and to the Pentagon's G2. The Pentagon G2 is much higher in rank than the division commander.

3. In AT&T before the dissolution, this structure was very strong. AT&T, however, was a regulated monopoly not subject to the discipline of vigorous competition.

4. Unless, of course, just by accident it happens that the division manager is an engine designer himself.

5. The more spectacular methods of execution used in China were not applied to officials, but losing their head was certainly a straightforward possibility.

6. This even applied to the very senior members of the censorate itself. Any censor had the right to send a sealed package that could be opened only by the emperor himself. Thus no one, not even the Board of Censors itself, could actually block criticism.

7. The Comptroller General is an attempt to create a similar control for the federal government. It works well for accounting, but when it gets out of simple accounts, we only get certain civil servants' opinions about what other civil servants are doing.

8. Grant was removed from command by Halleck the day after Shiloh because he had failed to file a morning report the day before. Lincoln reinstated him.

9. When I first joined the Foreign Service in 1948, we had two volumes of "regulations," and my superiors and other people who had been there for some time were rather unhappy because it had previously been one volume. By the time I left in 1958, there were 12 or 15 such volumes. They were kept in the administrative section, not anywhere where the higher officials in the embassy would find them convenient. As far as I know, they actually had effect only on the accounting branch of the embassy. Diplomacy does not lend itself very well to this kind of regulation, but nevertheless, I think that a short up-to-date set of regulations would have made it somewhat easier for people in Washington to exert what control they could over individual embassies.

10. This was only killing by Americans, of course. Many of them were cheering on the Vietminh.

11. Long ago, the customs service responded to a reduction in its budget by laying off every single customers inspector and not one single office employee. This was too much even for the Federal Government, and the civil servant responsible was transferred — not fired.

12. The censors normally left the magistrates alone. If they did leave the provincial capitals to visit the Hsiens, they might have been interested in more than just taxes and riots.

13. This depends on the dynasty and the time.

14. The Hsien frequently were located in portions of quite elaborate irrigation networks. In this case, there were other higher officials dealing with the irrigation network, but the Hsien magistrate would at least be expected to cooperate. Fortunately, this kind of activity in traditional China did not require much change from year to year. The use of the combined tax/no riot criteria nevertheless was a reasonably good measure of Hsien magistrate efficiency.

7 TERMITES

Long ago, I wrote a manuscript entitled "Coordination Without Command: The Economics of Insect Societies". If it had been published, it would have been the first book in sociobiology. The problem that has made sociobiology a controversial subject is the tendency of O. E. Wilson and his friends to draw lessons for humans from animal societies. I did not think that we should copy the ants and termites and I made a little restrained fun of an ant specialist who had talked in these terms. Perhaps I could have set sociobiology off on a better start, even though Wilson knows immensely more about insect societies than I do.

My reason for mentioning it is that I developed an economic theory as to how ant and termite nests succeed in coordinating their activities in spite of the fact that they have no central control, and the individual ants and termites have quite literally microscopic brains. This theory was, in essence, a radical generalization of standard market theory.[1] This radical generalization might be of some help in dealing with both private and governmental bureaucracies.

I assumed that ants and termites had very simple preference structures. For example, a given termite has a utility function that differs from ours only in the limited number of simple direct arguments in it. To take

89

only two, the termite "desires" both food and a reasonably well-repaired nest (the part of the nest with which he has immediate contact). Both of these desires are subject to declining marginal returns. When the termite attempts to maximize his satisfaction, he[2] either seeks food or repairs the nest, depending on which is most urgently demanded.

In actual practice, I would assume that the termites have 10 or 12 arguments in their preference functions. Nevertheless, the termite attempts to maximize this function which means that whichever of these arguments happens to have the highest marginal utility at the moment is the one it turns to. Thus, if the termite happens to be in a part of the nest that is in bad repair and has just eaten, it will repair the nest. If, on the other hand, it is in a part of the nest that is in good repair and is hungry, it will seek food.

Needless to say, the actual pattern of behavior is much more complicated; hence, the preference function must also be similarly complicated. But the system permits explanation of how a decentralized decision-making procedure, provided that the preferences are properly arranged, leads to highly coordinated behavior.[3]

It can be seen immediately that the standard discussion of market procedures is another example of the same kind of thing. We assume that human beings have a number of arguments in their preference function, all of which are subject to declining marginal returns; hence, they are apt to turn to the most pressing one. The basic difference between humans and termites is that humans are able to take indirect measures to meet their preferences. If we find that our front sidewalk is in a bad state of repair, we will very rarely drop everything else and begin fixing it. Usually we will undertake some other activity that permits us to earn money which we use to hire someone to repair it. Still, as I said, these two procedures have a family resemblance.

But not only the market. Public Choice assumes that people in politics also behave in this way. Politicians are motivated by a desire to maximize their preference function and take actions that rather indirectly are intended to that end, and the voters do the same. The basic differences among human beings are different preference functions and different abilities to produce outcomes which directly or indirectly meet those preference functions.

Among the ants and termites, however, if my theory is correct, then the preferences are pretty much identical unless the particular insect happens to have a caste system, in which case they are identical within each caste.[4]

I also think that bureaucrats are like this. They engage in various ac-

tivities in order to maximize their preferences and they observe the outside environment and take the activity which directly — or in human
beings, indirectly — is aimed at making that environment more in accordance with their wishes. At this radical level of generality, a termite who
observes something wrong with a tunnel in which it is moving and stops
to repair it, is behaving much the same as the bureaucrat who, fearing the
budget of his division will be cut next year, produces a minor crisis which
is intended to circumvent its occurrence.

The point of this digression is to argue that we can control bureaucrats
and, indeed, other people by means other than simply giving them orders.
We change their environment. I do not want to allege that an order does
not change the environment. Indeed, I was a bureaucrat myself and in a
service where travel orders sometimes changed my environment most
radically.

That is not the only way in which the environment can be changed.
For most human beings the most important part of the environment is
other human beings, and they are not necessarily your superiors. Even if
they are, they may have chosen to change your environment in some indirect manner rather than simply giving you an order.

Rules enforced by the regular police may be important in bureaucracies. At the time of this writing[5] the managers of the AEC are discovering
that just because they are federal employees does not protect them from
the FBI.[6] Thus, people organizing large-scale structures have alternatives
to direct orders. Unfortunately, these alternatives, although in many ways
highly efficient, are also hard to manipulate with precision.

It is also possible to change people's preferences so that they do what
the people at the head of the organization want. Military organizations
always devote much attention to what they call "morale" which, in essence, is an attitude of mind intended to lead soldiers into behavior that
is radically different from what we would normally expect. In modern
ground warfare with the units widely dispersed, this is particularly
important.

The market is an intermediate situation in which the person's direct
personal motives are adjusted to the desires of the overarching hierarchy
by providing a set of rewards or punishments. In America, for example,
most higher executives have their compensation tied one way or another
to the performance of their particular branch of the business. There are
many problems with these reward systems which will be discussed below;
nevertheless, they are an example of adjusting the environment so that
the individual does what you want without direct orders.

Perhaps it is easiest to discuss this environmental correction by begin-

ning with the preference function and efforts to adjust it. Adjusting it is
extremely difficult. All of the communist states devoted large-scale efforts
to producing the new Soviet, Chinese, and Cuban man. In all cases, the
moment the pressure relaxed, it turned out that they had failed. The large-
scale welcoming of the invading German troops[7] in Russia is one example.
The upsurge of severe criticism of the communist system that has occurred under Gorbachev is another example.

This chapter is being written immediately after the announcement of
the results of the first Polish election. The Polish Communist Party, apparently under the impression that it had succeeded in indoctrinating the
Poles, made a deal which, although certainly by no means a free election,
nevertheless gave Solidarity some power. The result was a catastrophe
for the Polish Communist Party which was not able to get its candidates
elected even in constituencies where there were was no opponent.[8]

Also at the time that this chapter is being written, the students in Bei-
jing are being repressed quite bloodily after they demonstrated that although the bulk of them are children of communist officials and although
they are undeniably the elite of the present government, they do not like
it. It would be hard to produce better evidence that the indoctrination
process, even over many years and accomplished by very skilled people,
can fail.

But if these systems have failed, there are other systems that work, at
least most of the time and when not subject to too great a pressure. De-
signers of such systems are well advised to see to it that first, not too
much strain is put on these indoctrinated preferences and, second, that
there be something in the environment that tends to reduce the strain by
rewards and punishments. Stalin understood this; in his case, and in the
case of Castro and the Chinese, elaborate methods were put in place to
punish those who deviated. In general, Communists put much more emphasis on the stick than on the carrot.

Indeed, the current difficulties in both China and Russia, and Poland
as well, have arisen because the mechanisms for providing penalties had
lost their bite. The higher officials themselves had forgotten how the system was intended to work and did not order out the troops and secret
police early enough. The fall of the Shah of Iran was caused by the same
error.

Pitiless repression will keep almost any group down, and making a lot
of concessions may work out reasonably well. Alteration between concessions and repression, however, which was the policy of the Shah, is very
dangerous, particularly if, as with the Shah, the repression is rather mildly
and inconsistently applied.[9]

But this is a discussion of the reward-and-punishment system rather than the changing preferences or more general environmental construction. Preferences do differ from one culture to another, and most governments make strong efforts to indoctrinate their subjects with whatever preference they think is desirable. The Chinese empire was perhaps the longest lasting example, dating back to the Chin Dynasty 2000 years ago. The indoctrination imposed through the educational system (by way of examinations[10] — they did not directly control the schools) in an elaborate philosophy and knowledge of government was, on the whole, very effective. It is notable, however, that although corruption was theoretically objected to, almost all officials were corrupt.

Consider, for example, *A Complete Book Concerning Happiness and Benevolence: A Manual for Local Magistrates in Seventeenth-Century China.*[11] This thick book, which went through a number of editions, was a sort of standard guide for officials who ran counties in China. It does not offer any direct advice on corruption but does discuss ways to keep down the tax payments to your provincial government. It also complains about various obviously corrupt acts by officials other than the head of the county government. Presumably, the readers of the book were able to carry out their corrupt activities on their own without the guidance of the book. Indeed, if the author had offered any advice on this topic, he would have met a sticky end.

Once again, there is no doubt this had effects. The duties of the officials, particularly the censors, included offering criticism to the emperor of the emperor's own conduct. This was a dangerous task, especially because a memorandum criticizing the emperor ritually ended with a request that the memorialist be executed for his impertinence. The emperor sometimes honored that request.

As another example, the Wanli Emperor, one of the less competent emperors in the later Ming, wanted more than almost anything else to make the son of his favorite concubine his heir rather than his eldest son. It stirred up so much objection from his officials that he did not dare do it even though he violated many other canons for the behavior of the emperor.

In modern structures, similar indoctrination is normal. Efforts are made to indoctrinate people into the policies of the post office or of Smith's supermarket, and our society as a whole has fairly strong procedures for indoctrinating people into its moral code.

Modern educationalists claim that one should not impose moral codes on people, but the only thing that has changed is the moral code they are imposing. The switch from "Homosexuals are unspeakable villains" to

"You may not criticize them and they have a right to live life as they choose" is a change in the nature of the moral system, not an abandonment of morals.

People frequently carry out these changed or imposed preferences when it would not be to their advantage. On occasion we read of someone who found a substantial amount of money and returned it to its original owner instead of just pocketing it. Not all students cheat even when doing so is fairly easy.[12]

Thus, higher-ups in organization normally have a modicum of control over the preference function of their subordinates. The society in which both the higher-ups and the subordinates operate has more but, again, not complete control. This can make organizing a bureaucracy easier.

We turn now to a way of changing the environment so that the individual is motivated to do the right thing without specific instructions. Another example of this point is an individual's obeying instructions when he/she does not really have to.

The whole elaborate mechanism of economics is a description of how people are led "as by an indivisible hand" to work for the advantage of other people, not because they are good but because the environment is so designed that their own goals will best be met by it. As Adam Smith said, our bread is provided by the baker, not because he has our interests in mind but because he has his own. This environmental coordination is, of course, not perfect. Monopolists are also responding to their environment.

Although the freely functioning market is an example of environmentally coordinated activity, people do not automatically develop efficient markets. Historically, many societies have put their reliance on other institutions. The market cannot simply be left alone to go as it wishes. Careful design, with periodic alternations, is necessary if we want to optimize. Unfortunately, most historic governments have not optimized, and their intervention in market process has often been undesirable. This should not imply that the market by itself operates perfectly.

What happens in the market is that my acts change the environment for other people and thus lead them to do things which, if I have performed properly and if the institutions are right, benefit me as well as them. The market is not the only place where this kind of coordination occurs. If Smith's opens a new supermarket in Tucson, it immediately changes the shopping environment for many people. Smith's happens to be well managed and intends to make money out of this expansion, but its success depends on the environment in which it operates and on other people's attitudes.

The concept of environmental coordination is not usually mentioned in regard to the market. In discussing it here, I am producing a somewhat different but nevertheless perfect mapping of the standard explanation, as the economists will realize.

Human beings have a fairly elaborate preference function, together with considerable calculating ability, which makes it possible for them to use indirect means to meet their most urgent preferences. Like the termite, however, their action is coordinated insofar as it is directly market-oriented by the fact that they observe the environment around them and take action calculated[13] to meet their more urgent needs.

Of course, because human beings have more complicated brains than termites, they may have a large collection of needs in mind and take actions intended to maximize this complex bundle, with each one treated in terms of its relative urgency. Taking a job, for example, provides an opportunity to meet many different arguments of the preference function, and the individual knows that. It is dubious that the termite is able to engage in this kind of complex reasoning.

Nevertheless, if we consider a pure market in which a group of farmers, say, trade with each other — a situation found even today in some primitive areas and which in the past was the dominant form of trade — we quickly realize that the farmers' behavior is an effort to maximize their own well-being by acts that are rather similar to those of the termites, although the latter do not ever engage in direct trade.[14]

From this kind of direct trade to the complex types of indirect trade of the modern world, the individual's market-dominated activity is still environmentally coordinated. The decision of Smith's market to stock a certain type of tropical fruit depends on its estimate of an important part of its environment, that is, the tastes of its customers. Shoppers regard the environment in which purchases are made as an important guide for their behavior.

The two "sides" each regard the other as part of the environment, and the coordination takes the form of changing the environment in order to get advantages in the long term. The difference between this and the termite nest is the greater complication of the preference function and the ability of human beings to engage in complex calculations beyond that of the termite.

Environmental coordination occurs in other than direct market operations of the purchase and sale type. The internal structure of any large organization can also be regarded as an example of environmental coordination, especially when superiors give orders and use the carrot and stick on inferiors. If I promise an inferior of mine that for accomplishing a certain task he will get a bonus, and for not doing it he will get fired, I have changed the environment in which that man operates. He then obviously has the choice of either doing as I say or departing.[15]

Whether this is a convenient way of talking about the matter is an open question, but there are parts of the environment not subject to direct order or supervision by a superior; these are important within an organization. In the first place, simple physical differences make certain types of action easy and other types difficult. All corporations try to establish physical boundaries to make it difficult for employees to steal anything.

Even the location of an office may have a considerable impact on what an individual does. Location affects the people you see and the information flow you receive through informal channels. The equipment an individual is provided may decidedly change his productivity, and the intellectual climate can also have its effects.

Also critical is the accounting system used. The Russians have had immense difficulty over the years in utilizing accounting systems that are not profit oriented. As mentioned previously, the effort to use physical "success indicators" has led to all sorts of severe difficulties. A *Crocodile* cartoon showed a nail factory facing a weight success indicator producing in the course of the year one gigantic spike. The following year it was given a number of nails criteria, producing an immense number of almost microscopic nails.

The fact that environmental coordination is one way of describing what goes on in the market and in corporations does have some real consequences because it reflects on the type of organization we see. With the extreme breadth of different organization types, we do not observe any single most efficient method of organizing the economy in different areas.

There do exist rare pure market transactions between individuals who work entirely on their own.[16] Here we have pure market environmental coordination. More commonly these days people are involved in some larger structure whether that structure is the government of the United States or the Ace Hardware Store franchise arrangement.[17] The spectrum of such organizations is absolutely immense. Corporations may be highly authoritarian in their organization. One example is the Japanese Just in Time automobile factories.[18]

Henry Ford probably had the largest organization with highly authoritarian structure. With his gigantic assembly line, everyone had to behave in exact accordance with the rules, or the assembly line would stop.[19]

I am involved in a minimal way with a small corporation in Iowa that makes clothing. Most of its employees are engaged either in cutting cloth or sewing different pieces of it together. These activities must be closely coordinated with what we can sell since we have many different styles, sizes and colors. Although the coordination is carried out first by a computer, this computer can be overridden by the higher officials and sometimes is. Nevertheless, the individual working in this plant has specific instructions as to what to cut or what exact two pieces of cloth to sew together with what kind of stitch.[20]

In this case, the coordination takes the form of instructions regarding what work material to place at the elbow of the person sewing and what its disposition will be. In most cases, the sewing machine operator does not receive any oral or written instructions, just a pile of a dozen or so clothing parts to put together.[21]

Environmental coordination occurs in many organizations where an unforeseen emergency is developing. Under these circumstances, personnel may respond to their previous training, but events will occur too fast for them to receive formal instructions.

This could be an enemy attack on a military unit or a machine breakdown in a factory, or an office facing a major increase in the potential workload. In all cases the environmental coordination is apt to be succeeded shortly by direct orders from above. Still, there will be a period in which the individuals make their own decisions which depend on the environment, including what other people are doing.

In the old days when fires were extinguished by volunteer fire departments, men would turn up at a fire and begin pumping water without any central control. It was thought to be a sort of contest in which the different independent fire companies[22] attempted to establish reputations by outdoing each other. Nevertheless the fire, the water sources and the location of the other fire companies involved were the main considerations of a fire company arriving on the scene; central control was not relevant.

I am not arguing that this is an ideal system, but then neither are the ants and termites. However, the latter have no other alternative; their system is the only one they have. Human beings can use other arrangements — for example, the carrot and stick for the market. Individuals being environmentally coordinated only insofar as environment determines where they will get rewards and where they will be driven into bankruptcy. On the other hand, we can use authoritative central instruction as, for example, in an army.

Universities are an almost perfect example of environmental coordination. Once a professor has been hired and receives tenure, the university can do little to control him. Indeed, it is a violation of ethics for the university to investigate what he is teaching. People who are actually mildly insane are permitted to continue teaching.[23]

The strength of this ethic in the universities is best demonstrated by another somewhat odd circumstance. When I was at the University of South Carolina, the school of business had contracted an accountant who practiced in downtown Columbia to teach a course in tax accounting. One morning he did not show up for class; he had been arrested for violation of the income tax law on his personal tax form.

The following day I was talking with several other faculty members, including his immediate superior in the school of business, about the fact that the department head had done nothing about relieving this person from his teaching responsibility. The department head was indignant at the suggestion that he do anything about the matter. Whether he would have continued paying the man's salary while in prison we do not know; as it turned out, he was only fined and continued teaching until his contract ran out. Whether arrest is grounds for dismissal is a contingency not usually considered in drawing up a contract. Nevertheless, the department head's indignation indicates the kind of ethical drive.

What, then, does lead professors to teach whatever they teach? They receive a number of cues from the environment and they follow them. They certainly are not subject to any strong control by the carrot and stick method or by orders from their superiors. Environmental coordination is strong enough, however, that many professors do not realize just how free they are.

The other aspect of academic life — research — is a clearcut case of environmental coordination, although here it is reinforced by some carrots. I submit an article to a journal over which I have no control whatsoever and which has no direct control over me; either they do or do not publish it. If they do, it is read by various people who regard it either as good or not. Clearly, this is an environmental factor. The university, however, regards the number of articles I have published and the prestige of the journals in which they appear as evidence in determining my salary level. Normally, the bright young faculty member is well advised to pay less attention to his/her teaching duties and more attention to writing articles to get ahead in the academic world.

Environmental coordination can lead to bad performance as well as good performance. Indeed, all social insects are subject to various problems in which the environmental coordination causes them to die off and the whole nest is destroyed. Certain circumstances can lead bees, ants or termites to respond to an environmental stimulus in a destructive way. Of course, if this happened very often that particular set of genes would be eliminated by evolution.

The same is true of human beings. I think environmental coordination "just grew" in the case of the academic environment, but in many other cases it is carefully designed and imposed. We should not assume that environmental coordination is a solution, nor should we assume that the carrot and stick or the system of direct orders is ideal. People, as many courtiers in the past have discovered, can win great rewards for action that is contrary to the interest of the king. Strict obedience to orders may on occasion lead to disaster for the person giving the orders.

Notes

1. I have another radical generalization to cover science in *The Organization of Inquiry*, (Durham, N.C.: Duke University Press, 1965; and Lanham, MD: University Press of America, 1987).

2. Or she. Unlike members of the wasp family like bees and ants, the termite workers can be either sex. They also have a royal pair instead of simply a queen. The mole rats, a social mammal, follow the wasps in having only a queen and female workers.

3. In both the ant and termite kingdoms there is a small amount of central control — from the queen in the case of the ants, and the royal pair or the royal group for termites — through the release of various chemicals. These chemicals control, however, a very small part of the total behavioral repertoire of these insects.

4. All of them have at least male and female and many have sexually nonfunctional working classes.

5. June 7, 1989.

6. The AEC management of the Rocky Flats plant are accused of various failures connected with the disposal of radioactive waste. I have no idea whether these accusations are true.

7. They made themselves unpopular over time but it is still true that large numbers chose to flee with them rather than to remain behind and face the Red Army.

8. It has been a rather odd characteristic of "elections" in communist countries that it is necessary to get 50 percent of the votes out for each election in order to have the unopposed candidate (traditional for communists) elected. Occasionally less than 50 percent would turn out even under Stalin and there would normally be complaints at this point about the poor organization of the election. In Poland, it was not that there was a small turnout, it was that the people crossed the communist name off the ballot. In this case, the peculiar communist method of election turned against them. They were hoist by their own petard.

9. The Shah had called in the International Red Cross to prevent his secret police from torturing suspects about two years before he was overthrown. The work of the Red Cross was not instantly effective, but there was almost no one tortured in the 18 months before his overthrow. This was nice, but dangerous.

10. Formal examinations are only about 1,000 years old, but the selection process in earlier years depended on much the same criteria.

11. By Huang Liu-Hung, translated and edited by Djang Chu, (Tucson, University of Arizona Press, 1984).

12. For evidence as to the quantity of cheating that one gets when it becomes easy, see Richard McKenzie and Gordon Tullock's *The New World of Economics* (Irwin) chapter on cheating, lying and fraud.

13. The termite does not calculate and engages in direct action.

14. Among both the termites and the ants, there is a transfer of food from some of them to others. This can be regarded as a trade but only by quite difficult mental gymnastics. If one observes an ant who has returned from a hunting expedition outside the nest and whose crop is full of food, meeting an ant whose principal duties are within the nest, one will observe them tapping antenna and then the hunting ant will regurgitate some food for the other ant. It can be called a trade in the sense that the ant bringing the food "pays" for the tapping with food, but I think it is more accurate to refer to this as the ant coming in having an argument in its utility function in which delivering food to other ants is something that is positive and valuable. It lays off against the advantages of that particular preference the advantages of consuming the food itself, and takes whichever is most urgent.

15. Rommel, when a mere temporary company commander, once gave a platoon leader the choice of obeying orders or being shot on the spot. This changed his environment radically (*Attacks* by Field Marshal Erwin Rommel, Provo, Utah: Athena Press, 1979, p. 67). Although the publishers give Rommel his eventual rank, at the time he wrote the book he was a lieutenant colonel.

16. As one example, an attorney I used to know had a client who was an inventor of gadgets. Although the attorney had a secretary, he operated on his own and the inventor depended primarily on inspiration rather than hiring a lot of assistants.

17. We remember in this case that the franchising runs backwards. The "owners" of the stores own the franchising organization.

18. The particular scheme is currently breaking down with a lot of subcontracting.

19. A number of other large-scale production operations behave almost exactly the same way.

20. The stitch is predetermined by the fact that the individual workers use specialize sewing machines. Normally one worker will always sew the same kind of stitch because that is the kind of machine he/she has. The computer directs the work to the appropriate worker as well as telling the worker what to do.

21. The scheme which sounds a priori inefficient and looks inefficient in the factory, comes from the extraordinary flexibility that is necessary in a textile operation. The factory holds inventory for the retailers who order small bundles of different sizes, colors, and models for immediate delivery rather than maintaining an inventory of their own. Under the circumstances, long machine runs of a particular size, color, and style of, say, shorts are less economic than this system of a larger number of short runs. At the moment, there are no machines that have anywhere near the flexibility of the human being for this kind of an operation.

22. It should be pointed out that the pumping water in this case was a matter of human muscle and so in a way it was an athletic contest.

23. The subject matter as specified in the catalog is controlled, but I have known at least two cases in which professors came to the conclusion that that subject matter was not really important and simply taught courses in other subjects. In one, a conservative and slightly off-his-rocker individual decided that the standard course in statistics, al-

though no doubt of some rudimentary interest, should be replaced by another course he had written and which no one other than himself had ever succeeded in understanding.

The other case came during the unpleasantness of the late 1960s in which a professor teaching a course in neurophysiology completely dropped that topic and simply discussed politics with his students. Since he gave all the students an A, the course was immensely popular.

Neither of these individuals was fired nor subjected to any disciplinary activity. The first one, in fact, eventually was given an honorary position.

8 A GENERAL PICTURE

Consider any society. We find that within it many of the possible human interactions do not exist; for example, I have no contact whatsoever with any man living in San Francisco. Among the social interactions that do exist, many are quite casual and do not take up much time; others are more important. Of the important ones, some are direct bargains in which something is traded for money, products, service, and so on.

Many others, however, are long-lasting relationships in which the same people have contact with each other over time. Of these, many are simple contractual relationships of the type you obtain when you buy a car on credit or when you enter into, as I have, a contract with a gardening company. Among this group, however, we will see cases in which a number of people are grouped together into permanent organization and in which the relations between them are not the result of bargaining. Although an employee can always quit and his employer can always fire him, while they are engaged in their cooperative endeavor, their relationship does not normally center around specific bargains about each individual step. Some nonhierarchical relationships have this same characteristic. I have mentioned my contract gardener, and on occasion I ask him to do something special or complain about something that he has done.[1]

Let us simplify this structure radically to begin our discussion of why we observe these different types of organization. Assume that we have a society where there are no monopolies and no externalities,[2] and in which, for reasons which we will not now discuss, property rights are maintained.

Since division of labor pays, we would anticipate that different people would be producing different things and would engage in exchanges. Our experience indicates that there are economies of scale in many types of activities; hence, that for many activities, large hierarchical organizations would exist, and there would be a whole set of small hierarchical organizations at different levels of economies of scale. There is no reason that this type of operation could not develop quite spontaneously from people simply wanting to maximize their well-being with some people choosing to organize lots of others into large organizations, other people choosing to work in the large organizations for salaries, and still others remaining as independent operators.

In any existing corporation, people can be divided into four categories. First and absolutely vital are the customers who, for some obscure reason, tend to be left out in the usual discussion; second, the workers, and the workers are normally broken into managerial and nonmanagerial types, with the people at the top frequently called entrepreneurs. In the final category, we have the people who put up the capital.

There is no intrinsic reason why the fourth category has to be separate. If one looks at the average American corporation, the employees, if they put their entire personal wealth (equity in their house, insurance policy, car, and so on) into the pot, could buy control of the corporation. If they do not, the apparent reason is that they are risk-averse. "Don't put all your eggs in one basket" is a sensible bit of folk wisdom.

As an aside, I should point out that there are employee-owned firms. The case most discussed in economic literature is the law firm, which is unusual because it does not have much nonhuman capital. The present-day large law firm, a recent invention, apparently is a byproduct of the extraordinarily complicated law which has developed in recent years. It provides specialists for each particular branch of the law so customers do not need to track down suitable specialists themselves. In systems where the law is simpler and an individual lawyer can know the whole law himself, these big organizations are not needed.

The other cases of employee-owned firms fall roughly into three categories. One is the small group of cases in which a wealthy man has died and bequeathed his enterprise to its employees, a system that usually does not last very long. Parallel to it are a few cases in which the company itself has had bad luck and has lost a large part of its equity value. If the cause of its loss is a powerful union that has kept wages above the equilibrium level, then transferring the company to the union may be a convenient way of lowering the wages.

The final case is the rare situation where a company has actually developed under employee ownership. The plywood cooperatives that used to be so important on the West Coast are examples, but they, like the others, are tending to disappear. Their basic problem, from the owner-operator standpoint, is that they are risky investments. Understandably, these people would prefer to be employed by one firm and put their money into something else.[3]

A certain number of people do start corporations, investing all their money into it. As an extreme example, Roy Kroc in his fifties sold a small company that he owned and put that capital together with an immense amount of work on his own part into what must have seemed an extremely long-shot gamble. Of course, McDonald's paid off. Most of the businessmen who do this, and it is not too rare, lose their shirts. We are fortunate that a considerable number of people in our society are willing to take this kind of risk.

In most cases, however, the capital is provided by a separate group of people who not are actually employed by the firm although some higher managers may possess considerable capital.

In family corporations, some of which still exist, some substantial stockholders may be members of the lower management. These are young men starting in the business and learning it from the bottom up.

Looking at the world, then, we observe a number of large organizations engaged in, say, manufacturing and selling automobiles. In addition, there are a number of individuals working entirely on their own and in all of the intermediate stages. There are also governmental organizations, but by (temporarily) ruling out externalities, we have in large part made them unnecessary.[4]

The relationship of these large groups to exterior groups is also important. In a real sense, customers act as an important police force for the efficiency of any firm. Only if the firm can produce and sell its products at a price that permits covering all costs, preferably with something left over, can it continue to exist. Another police force is the employees. They must be paid a wage and be provided with working conditions so that they will want to stay.

Last, the capital providers — which in our society are normally separate from those two groups but could be melded with either one[5] — must all be satisfied by this entity. This is different from the individual operator working on his own who can accept low personal returns if he wants. This large entity cannot afford to provide output that is of poor quality or too high in price, to provide wages and working conditions to its employees that are less than competitive, or to produce a return on capital below that of its competitors. It is subject, then, to fairly stern disciplinary activity. Again, this does not require any government activity although government is also important in the real world.

The management must make the decisions and carry out general policy directives in this organization. The problem of making certain that everyone is working hard and trying to do their best is, as Alchian and Demsetz have correctly argued, best left to the residual claimant. The problem with this is that anyone can be the residual claimant. In most American corporations, the profits of the corporation go to the stockholders who are the residual claimants, but there are other possible organizations.

An obvious case is a worker-owned firm where the workers are the residual claimants, and we do occasionally find situations in which the customers are the residual claimants. One such case is the consumer cooperative; we earlier mentioned the rather peculiar organization of Ace Hardware in which the individual stores were customers of the central franchising and wholesaling organization and were also the residual claimants. In each of these cases, the residual claimants are legally the people who have control.

Traditionally, there was a situation in which bankers, who simply loaned money to the corporation, were the people in control. The House of Morgan in 1900 was one example. During that period, a lot of the money was invested on the reputation of the bank rather than the reputation of the company. It seems likely, however, that the bankers themselves made their decisions in terms of the size of the equity held by the common stockholders. If it was large, the company was worth more loans; if it was small, it was not, and the management had better be changed.

Why in most cases do the stockholders have the ultimate right to fire the management? It isn't so in management-controlled firms, but among established firms, management control is comparatively rare. The answer, I think, is simple. The stockholders, a group of people who know little about the corporation, pay little attention to it and can easily get out of the corporation by selling their stock; are almost the only ones whose activities cannot possibly be at fault for the corporation's poor functioning.

One reason the corporation is not doing well might be that it is paying its workers too much, and the workers would hardly fire the management for that. Similarly, the corporation might be charging too low a price to its customers who would also not fire the management. The management itself, almost by definition, is likely to be satisfied with its own behavior and will not fire itself. The stockholders normally do nothing whatsoever about the corporation except to change the management occasionally. Their sole interest lies in the company's profitability, and they do not have the same conflicts of interest as all the other possible final claimants.

Another aspect to consider is that the stockholders are apt to be relatively lacking in risk aversion. Insofar as they are risk-averse, they can diversify their investment; therefore, they are usually willing to make sizeable gambles on any individual stock. Furthermore, their effect on the organization of the corporation can be registered by simply unloading the stock that they think is doing badly or by voting against the corporation. In the past, corporations sometimes faced proxy fights to get rid of the management; now they face takeovers. The takeover is a better method provided that the financial market is organized well enough to assemble the money for it. Apparently, this last condition has only recently been met.

In any event, the management itself is apt to respond to threats of either a proxy fight or a takeover by making changes within its structure. The efforts of management in recent years — unfortunately, very successful — to protect themselves against either form of discipline, and in particular against the takeover bid, are no doubt reducing the efficiency of our system. It is a case in which supervision is clearly failing.

But to say that supervision is failing because the managers are beginning to protect themselves against being thrown out for inefficiency[6] raises a question about the general supervision. The corporation stockholders normally have to approve these various measures or, alternatively, the measures are enacted by a legislature in which the corporation stockholders certainly have more potential influence than the management does.[7] It seems simply to be poor supervision. Most stockholders, because they can readily switch from one company to another, are relatively uninterested in the management of a particular company.

If the supervision is failing and a proxy fight (the older technique) develops, stockholders can probably decide casually which way to vote, and that necessarily puts the management under pressure. In the more modern method, the takeover fight is a good way of making money.[8] In this method, the stockholder, by selling their stock, depress its price; some "pirate" buys the company, fires the present management and replaces it with a better one, then sells the company again with a potential capital gain.

All of this indicates that stockholder supervision is decidedly less than optimal if we think not of the well-being of the stockholders but of society as a whole. However, if we rearranged the corporation so that the residual claimant was the workers, the customers or the management itself,[9]the situation would be worse. Furthermore, if we consider the utility of the stockholders as part of the value for society, their decision not to spend much time on the job of supervising may more than pay for the inefficiency of that supervision.

So far we have been talking about the environment that surrounds the corporation and how it polices the efficiency of the corporation. We have not talked about the hierarchy itself which starts at the top with the management and works its way down through the workers. That hierarchy faces a difficult task because it is subject to severe competition.

In government the competition is much less thorough. Also, competition in government is not always aimed at a socially desirable goal. The competition of different companies for customers means they are under continuous pressure to cut prices and improve quality. The competition for laborers means that they are pressured to improve conditions at work and raise wages. Finally, the competition that they face to keep the stockholders satisfied and arrange to borrow money from the banks, making certain that the net value of the stockholders' equity is sizeable, tends to make capital in society invest in its most highly valued use.

In other types of activity — government and nonprofit organizations — these pressures are much weaker. Thus, the government and the nonprofits operate in a less vigorously controlled environment, and one can anticipate that they will not work as well.

Even though in this book we concentrate on government and private profit-making bureaucracies, there are other bureaucracies in our society such as the nonprofit portion in which I work.[10] In general, the nonprofits are small organizations. Even if we consider Harvard University, its size is trivial compared to a moderate-sized corporation. It does not have a large bureaucracy, but it sometimes behaves in a bureaucratic way. Custom and individual preferences of employees seem to be its primary controlling variables.

Nonprofit organizations can, however, operate under highly controlled circumstances. The current legal problems of the Jim Bakker family come from the fact that they set up a large nonprofit organization and diverted its revenue to management prerequisites. Granted the objectives they had, it was efficient. What we object to are the objectives.

In general, the present organization of non-profits exists almost entirely to prevent money from being diverted in a similar way to that of the Bakkers. Certainly a self-perpetuating board is not likely to be an efficient organization particularly if its members are selected primarily in terms of their ability to raise money rather than for their knowledge of the subject matter.

Most of my readers and I have been for a long time in organizations governed in this way. Most state university boards are not self-perpetuating but are selected by the government of the state in terms of whether they have reasonably good political connections but are not actually candidates for anything. This gives us people similar to those, say, on the board at Harvard, except, our people do not have as much money. Since they have considerable influence on the state legislatures, however, the net effect is that they provide more money to the university than the board does to Harvard.

To repeat, these nonprofits do not operate particularly efficiently. Their tax-exemption, together with the fact that they are able to get free or cheap labor because of their charitable names, could make them able to compete successfully with regular business. Bennett and DiLorenzo have, in fact, written a book on the subject.[11] Nevertheless, it is hard to argue that this is a good system; also, it has no true residual claimant.

Consider the standard art museum. It benefits a considerable number of members of the upper class who like to visit it, regard it as a social center, and so on. It also probably benefits a certain number of the lower class individuals who have artistic desires and can get them filled cheaply.[12] A number of middle-class housewives whose children have gone off to school find useful activities around the museums such as running the museum shop. If they are wealthy they may be on the board. But these people are not the residual claimants despite their probable influence on the management.

Ultimately, the influential people are those in a position to provide further funding. A board member who is thinking vaguely of giving the museum a Rembrandt is a man whose every word is listened to with baited breath. But neither are these people residual claimants; in a way, they are residual sources of money.

The staff in nonprofit organizations has much more influence than in a private corporation simply because the objectives are not as clearcut and measurable as they are in a private corporation. It is not true that the people who visit the museum or the artsy-craftsy types who make up its board are as ignorant of the museum's affairs as the average stockholder is of his company. It is true, however, that the simple bookkeeping number that determines the success or failure of the company is brought to the attention of various people who might be interested — raiders, for example — where nothing like this happens at museums.[13]

When we have a scandal in a museum or church, then it is similar to the situation with the Bakkers in which money has actually been diverted to the management. Scandals in private companies normally take the form of irregular activities that the management undertook to increase the profit of the company, not to add to their own personal rakeoff.

Having said this, however, I should say that the lower part of the hierarchy in nonprofit organizations is usually not very closely supervised. Fortunately, it also is usually small since most of these organizations are not big. Although inefficient, there appears to be no better way.

In regard to a larger part of our society, the government, as mentioned previously, suffers from not having any clearcut measure of efficiency like accounting; but in a democracy it does have another measure — the number of votes it gets. This differs from the number of votes that the current management will get at the next election in a corporate organization because usually there is no opposition in the corporation. When there is, it frequently takes the form of some kind of intermittent pirating technique in which the existing management will be displaced.[14]

Furthermore, although the voter in a political election is typically badly informed, he/she is better informed than the common stockholder who is voting in a corporation. The last phenomenon is to some extent counterbalanced by the people and organizations whose stock holdings in a given corporation are large enough so that they do become informed. The corporate structure is designed so that ideally these people will act as proxies for the other common stockholders rather than using their power for diverting funds to themselves.

Here, again, we have a potential scandal that almost never occurs in the United States. All corporations with a true majority stockholder or stockholding family may in fact divert things like private cars for the corporate manager, and so on, to themselves at the expense of the minority holders. The degree to which they can do this without going to jail for embezzlement, however, is limited. A judge with a much lower personal income will decide whether the expenditure was a proper and ordinary. A car, trips to conventions, and some entertainment expenses are about all corporation members can safely claim.

Even officers of major corporations usually do not have this kind of option. Of course, various incentive plans are probably more generous to the management than it really deserves, but this generosity is limited. Besides, the stockholders benefit from the incentive plan because it gives managers greater motivation. Certainly, these procedures (which, under corporation law, have to be voted in by the stockholders) are usually endorsed. Presumably, the stockholders do not know anything about their particular corporation, but they do know that this technique is good.

In Europe corporate laws are different. There, cheating is common. Sometimes the people operating the corporation have succeeded in cutting out a lot of the other stockholders. The reason it does not occur in the United States is, oddly enough, because of a cartel restriction. In the days when the New York Stock Exchange had an effective monopoly, it imposed a single category of voting stock, which would be the residual legatee,[15] on all corporations who wanted their stock listed. The reason they did so was presumably to increase the attractiveness of the product. That is, they wanted to sell common stock widely because they were the principal market for it. The New York Stock Exchange has lost its monopoly status, but the effect of the rule is still strong.

Certainly, it is hard these days to sell stock that does not have such a system. When Henry Ford died, Ford Motor Company was left partly to the Ford Foundation in the form of a gigantic amount of nonvoting stock and partly in the form of a much smaller amount of voting stock to his direct heirs. Eventually, the corporation converted the nonvoting stock to voting stock to permit the Ford Foundation to sell it at a good price.

With government, the voters differ from the voters in a corporation in several ways. One is that there are no individuals with a whole pile of votes who are deeply interested in the outcome and who, therefore, may become well informed. During the period when England rose from the status of a rather backward island off the northwest coast of Europe to the world's dominant power, England did have a class of voters of this sort. The existence of the rotten borough system meant that there were a number of men who personally sat in the House of Lords but who owned enough seats in the House of Commons so that they could strongly influence the political activities of the government. They seem to have played somewhat the same role as the large individual stockholder does in companies even where he/she owns only, say, 3 percent of a gigantic corporation. This system is generally regarded as undemocratic.

In an ordinary democracy, then, the voter is slightly better informed than the voter in the corporation. He/she suffers from not having any simple way of telling if the government is working well or badly. The politician has a way of telling whether the government is working badly in the sense that he counts the votes. But these votes are votes of people who have no motivation to become informed, so it is not obvious that this index is positive.

The individual voter has another problem. There is normally a conflict of interest between him and society as a whole. Let us take an old example. After Athens recovered from the defeat of the Peloponnesian war, she began construction of a second "empire."[16] The standard historical account as to why this empire failed is that the Athenian government had developed the habit of making direct payments to the voters out of surplus funds. Since the voters decided what funds were surplus, they tended to underfund the navy and overfund their own pocketbooks. They were willing to pay for the navy when Athens was actually at war, but they were not willing to keep it up in peacetime. As a result, Athens never regained its naval prominence after the Syracusan expedition.

Other more recent examples include the farm program of almost any democratic country, the Central Arizona Project, and the Tombigee Canal. A particularly striking example is the reluctance of even pacifistically inclined congressmen to close military bases in their districts.

Again, for this phenomenon to be absent in corporations, the accounting system must be more than a simple profit-and-loss account. Individual stockholders no doubt would exert similar pressure on the corporation except that, fortunately, it is illegal and almost instantaneously detectable. Unfortunately, in democratic politics things are not so simple; hence, this kind of activity is common.

But why do we have government? Clearly, it is not a terribly efficient organization. However, in my opinion,[17] dictatorships are less efficient and less interested in the well-being of every citizen. The answer is that although the market can be highly efficient in certain areas, in other areas — where there are large externalities — it is highly inefficient.

The choice is between two types of instruments: one is intermittently efficient and the other is almost always mediocre. We should choose the market where it is efficient, and where it is less efficient than the mediocre government, we should chose the government.

I mentioned above that a traditional duty of the government is the enforcement of contracts and property rights. This task is allocated to the government. That is not because there is a great externality in that activity but maintaining a force on hand capable of this enforcement does generate externalities. Many of our legal decisions are handled by organizations called arbitral courts. The great Roman law was developed by a group of jurisconsults who held no government position. As a final example, the modern Roman-Dutch tradition depends on essays written by law professors rather than by courts or legislatures. Indeed, our law is frequently changed by nongovernmental officials engaging in some kind of educational activity aimed at legislatures or judges.

There is no reason why we should complain about this, but also no reason why we should argue that it is ideally efficient. If a number of groups undertook the forceful act of enforcing these decisions, however, there would be problems. For example, I could hire someone to dispossess a householder whom I alleged had not kept up the payments on his mortgage,and he could hire someone else because he alleges that he has. A small war would ensue. The current conditions in Lebanon indicate what one might expect from living for a number of years with that approach. Because our desire to avoid it is understandable, we try to keep the use of force in society restricted to one agency — a so-called monopoly of force — and consider it a sensible policy.

Of course, in the United States a number of different agencies can use force because the individual citizen is subject to several different levels of government. If I did not keep up the payments on my mortgage I would be dispossessed by a county official, the sheriff; if I speed, depending on where I am, I might be arrested either by a state policeman or a municipal policeman. If worse comes to worst and public order breaks down, the military can be called in.

If our two levels, the state and the federal government, do not get into war with each other, there is no great difficulty. The obvious small size of any given low-level organization as opposed to the central organization normally prevents that from happening but, of course, we did have the Civil War. The War of the American Revolution could also be used as an example where local governments decided to fight the central government.

The general picture here is that hierarchies are rather similar, whether they are government or private. The private hierarchies have an element of efficiency that makes measurement of their performance easier, more so than in the government. Certain people — corporate raiders, for instance — can make a great deal of money by discovering that one of these hierarchies is behaving inefficiently and by taking steps to improve it. Unfortunately, this is not characteristic of the government. The internal lives of the two organizations are quite similar, however. To re-quote William Niskanen: "Sociologically, there is no difference between the federal government and the Ford Motor Company".

What we have, then, is a society in which a large number of different organizations — some of them small, some of them simply individual people — are interacting. Our goal should be a structure in which the individual organizations are motivated to behave efficiently and the interaction is efficient. Over the history of the human race, these objectives have been a preoccupation of truly great minds, but it cannot be said that they have been finally solved.

Notes

1. Actually, it is not obvious in this case whether I should say he or she/he. My original contract was made with the wife of the man who right now is doing most of the supervision. The apparent explanation of the switch in the people I am dealing with has to do with a new baby.

2. Of course, many economists regard monopolies as an example of an externality generating activity.

3. For the average worker, that means a house.

4. Property enforcement and enforcement of contracts are traditional government activities, but in both cases it can be argued that their real reason for existing is externality reduction.

5. Consumer-owned cooperatives are not a very significant part of our economy, but they do exist.

6. This is not, of course, their explanation for why they are protecting themselves.

7. This would not be true with respect to any given corporation. Stockholders are spread all over the world while the management is concentrated in the headquarters state. But the total number of stockholders in any state will normally outnumber the total management, and these laws affect all corporations chartered by the state. In many cases, the headquarters is not in the chartering state at all.

8. One of the byproducts here is the development of the specialized industry in which a "pirate" threatens a takeover and gets paid a significant amount of green mail in order to not carry the threat out. The fact that the stockholders do not prevent the green mail payment is another example of poor supervision by the stockholders.

9. For a great many European corporations, particularly in France, the latter condition is true, and this may indicate why their economy is not really flourishing.

10. I am, of course, an employee of the state government, but the academic portion of our society, even though now largely dominated by the government, still continues to act in much the same way as it did 30 or 40 years ago when it was dominated by private organizations. In a way, it is a private nonprofit organization that depends on a state legislature rather than John D. Rockefeller for its economic support and gives about as much control to the legislature as Chicago did to John D. Rockefeller.

11. *Unfair Competition: The Profits of Nonprofits* by James T. Bennett and Thomas J. DiLorenzo (New York: Hamilton Press, 1989).

12. Actually, the members of the lower class normally are not much interested in such things. It is the upper class that goes into them. But, no doubt, some lower class people or poverty-stricken people do patronize these subsidized museums.

13. See Grampp, William Dyer, *Pricing the Priceless: Art, Artists, and Economics,* (New York: Basic Books, 1989); Frey, Bruno S. and Pommerehne, Werner W., *Muses and Markets: Explorations in the Economics of the Arts,* (Oxford: Basil Blackwell Ltd., 1989); and Banfield, Edward C., *The Democratic Muse: Visual Arts and the Public Interest* (New York: Twentieth Century Fund, Inc., 1984).

14. Sometimes with a golden handshake.

15. The development of warrants has to some extent made this no longer a true residual legatee arrangement. But the warrants are simply the right to buy common stock, so this makes no great difference.

16. "Empire" is not a very good description of the Athenian polity. The individual city-states that fell within it were self-governing and in most cases seem to have been quite happy about the whole arrangement. Many of them remained loyal to Athens even in the last desperate days of the Peloponnesian war.

17. I have written a book on dictatorships, *Autocracy*, (Dordrecht, Netherlands, Martinus Nijhoff, 1987).

9 RANDOM ALLOCATION

How do you control your subordinates? I have already discussed briefly methods of improving your control if you are striving for perfect control and have pointed out that you must be satisfied with less than perfect effectiveness of these methods. Accordingly, I will now discuss relaxing your requirements.

In trying to get as much control as possible, we will begin with a simple structure: one man at the top of a hierarchy has as his only objective getting his desires implemented. We will assume that at each stage of the hierarchy in our structure, each person supervises three people. Thus, our man at the top supervises three immediate assistants each of whom supervises three below that, and so on. We will also simplify matters by assuming that, at each level of the hierarchy, including the top person, individuals spend half their time determining what should be done and the other half seeing to it that their inferiors carry it out.

This last assumption is, I think, quite realistic. My experience with high officials indicates that they do make a lot of decisions on their own, an ability that is equally as important in determining their success as their ability to supervise inferiors. They frequently, of course, consider the advice of their inferiors in their decisions.

As mentioned earlier, the committees, or groups of administrators in large organizations, are the vehicles for producing new ideas and winnowing them down so that the ideas that reach the top are a favorable selection. Well-run organizations, however, do not simply accept the top recommendation of this administrative swamp. The higher official looks over several of the decisions, selecting the one that he likes best. Sometimes the individual at the top will invent his own idea rather than accepting the ones presented to him. Even in this case, however, he will usually turn to the administrative swamp for some processing of his basic idea.

For the time being, we will not regard this man as supervising the sources of information or ideas upon which he bases his decisions. He will simply divide his time equally between making up his own mind, seeing to it that his inferiors implement his desires.

This man's decisions constitute what we might call a general policy. He wants the people in the next step down to devote half of their time making up their minds about the detailed instructions for their subordinates, which are in accord with his basic ideas, and half in supervision. The same thing is true with each lower stage. We assume realistically that the orders from on high require elaboration and adjustment to special conditions in each division and the division head spends half of his time on that and the other half on supervision.

One thing the man at the top has to supervise, and which each supervisor down has to supervise as well, is the elaboration that is carried out during this half-time of decision-making by the lower-level officials.

To take a famous example, on the second day at Gettysburg, General Lee sent General Longstreet around his right to seize Little Round Top, which dominated the battlefield. But there was also the standing regulation in the armies of both the North and the South that troops march for 50 minutes and then take a ten-minute break.[1] Whether General Longstreet's corps should take their break exactly at the right time after precisely 50 minutes, or continue on for another few minutes to the top of the hill was clearly General Longstreet's decision. He decided to take the break. This decision was extremely important. Whether Lee would have won the battle if Longstreet had gone on is unknown, but Mead would certainly have been forced to realign his entire position.

Another aspect of this particular incident illustrates what can go wrong with a command structure. Little Round Top was saved for the Union by a quarter-master major-general who rode up to the top of the hill simply to look at the battlefield. He noticed Longstreet's forces coming up, dashed back, and succeeded in talking some local units not directly under his command into moving to the Little Round Top; thus, it was held.

When he arrived at the top, he found a signal corps observatory that was busily engaged in observing, using telescopes better than the ones he had, and sending messages somewhere by semaphore. Apparently, there had been a breakdown in the bureaucracy here or the general's intervention would not have been necessary.

We have here simply an example of the need for elaboration of orders. Had General Lee been physically present, he would have countermanded the ten-minute delay. But, again, one cannot be sure. In any event, it is necessary for each level as you go down the pyramid to decide, in some detail, what should be done with the orders from above. The guideline of using half the time for this activity simply makes the model easier to follow.

The problem I want to discuss here is how the supervisors allocate their time in the supervision part of their duties. They can only devote one-sixth of their time to each of the individuals under them, meaning that of necessity their supervision is imperfect.

In some cases, one-sixth is a perfectly adequate allocation of time. Until recently, military units in combat or in drill were arrayed in long, straight lines. The supervisors could easily and quickly tell how well the units were doing. Frederick the Great at Rosbach could see a large part of his army and a large part of the approaching French army. His lower-level commanders had an even better view of the particular troops under their command. Under these circumstances, an individual soldier who tried to hold back, or a regimental commander who was moving slowly, could assume that their activity was directly observed by their superior despite the large numbers of soldiers under them.

Even that was not perfectly simple. Generalship involved doing something your opponent did not anticipate, and that frequently meant that some of your troops would be out of his observation and also out of yours. Napoleon lost the Battle of Leipzig to a considerable extent because a portion of his army that he sent on a circuitous route around the flank miscarried.

Much depends, of course, on how easy the task is to supervise. The situation in the traditional army in which the soldiers stood in long, straight lines is unfortunately exceptional. As we have pointed out, at least the accounting system provides a way of telling whether people are achieving one narrow goal, making a profit. Unfortunately, it is imperfect because conditions surrounding each individual member of, say, the Safeway chain, are different than all the others.

Even in Frederick the Great's army a straight line of soldiers advancing might find the land inconsistent. Part of the line might be in deep mud while the rest might be on hard earth. But such problems are easier to

deal with than those involved in trying to decide whether two supermarket managers have different profit rates because of different levels
of efficiency or because of purely local conditions beyond their control.

One way of dealing with this, used pretty uniformly by large organizations, is to have policies that are easy to monitor and that are allegedly
efficient. For example, a number of supermarkets have a policy under
which their house brands, that is, brands they have produced for themselves and that normally have a somewhat higher profit margin, are to be
placed in the middle of a shelf, with the non-house brands, which they
have to carry in order to remain competitive with other supermarkets,
placed on either side. Supposedly, people are more likely to select the
house brands from there than they would be if they had been placed at
one end of the row. In any event, this is easy to check.

Other procedures are also easy to monitor, such as the continuous rotation of material on the shelves so that nothing exceeds its shelf life.
Matters such as these are usually handled by special inspectors of a lower
rank than district supervisors. Of course, the district supervisor will occasionally monitor their inspectors by checking shelves whenever they
are in the store.

Regulations also exist in higher-level areas. Most of the supermarket
chains have policies about such things as displays, which part of the mer-
chandise should be in what part of the store, and so on. The responsibility
for these adjustments reverts to the local manager since, for instance, the
floor space and layout vary at different stores.

In addition, certain Safeway stores are located in areas where the public's taste lies outside the mainstream, partly because of income level and
partly because of ethnic variation. I live in Tucson which has a very
substantial Mexican population and where the non-Mexican population
is attracted to Mexican food. If Safeway wants to make money, it must
adjust in this direction, deviating from what we might call national
standardization.

The military system of Frederick the Great is perhaps the easiest to
supervise of any government organization we know. Safeway, however,
is as close as we are likely to get in any large hierarchic organization. In
many cases, large organizations face vastly more complex problems.
Consider, for example, the management of a true conglomerate whose
subdivisions are engaged in radically different types of production. One
company may engage in making parts for air force planes, owning a couple of television stations or a chain of convenience stores, and perhaps
participating in a dozen other diverse areas. Not only must it obtain effi-

ciency within each of these divisions, it has to be able to supervise the divisions themselves, although they have nothing in common but the profit motive.

In government, the situation is much worse because the simple goal of making a profit is not there. In the United States, consider the President's immediate inferiors. He has a postmaster general, who engages rather ineptly in moving the mail around the country; a secretary of state, engaged in dealing with foreign nations; a secretary of the interior, who has a widely diverse collection of duties, mainly in the western part of the United States; the armed forces, one part of which (army engineers) does work similar to that of the Department of Interior in water projects; the Department of Justice which maintains prisons and acts as a lawyer for many government agencies. We could go on.

The President has no easy way to compare whether his attorney general is more or less efficient in carrying out his task than his secretary of the interior is. They do not have the same tasks. The situation is similar within other divisions. For instance, although the attorney general maintains prisons and a legal staff that does much of the government's legal work, his office also recommends judicial appointments and has half a dozen other activities which are only rather loosely related. Cabinet bureaus are similarly set up. In all of these cases, a supervisor must have some direct knowledge of a large variety of procedures and select from among them. Furthermore, if he does so, he must be certain that his judgement in the area is at least as good as that of the person he is supervising. If not, he may lower efficiency by his supervision rather than raise it. Obviously, he cannot do everything or know everything with which his subordinates deal, so he must make a selection.

The first problem confronting a supervisor, then, is what to supervise. Which aspects of his inferiors' work should he attempt to control? He does not want the inferior to be completely free to make decisions about everything except some small area that the supervisor checks regularly. He wants the inferior to do things which the supervisor would undoubtedly favor if he checked them. Because the superior will only check a small collection, this is difficult.

The method that automatically occurs to any economist considering this problem is random selection. Furthermore, an experienced supervisor's behavior does have some random components but is not perfectly random for reasons we will discuss below. Let us, however, consider a situation in which the supervisor is literally random in his choices. Again, our procedure involves three inferiors of the man at the top, each of whom supervises three, each of whom supervises three; we will stop at that point, with 27 people at the bottom actually taking action in the outside world, and the remainder being supervisors.

The superior now is devoting only one-half of his time to supervision; hence, he can devote only one-seventy-second of his time to each of his 36 inferiors if he allocates time evenly among them. Roughly speaking, he could give one day every three months to each. If they did not know what day that would be, they would be under considerable pressure to design their activities such that no matter what day it turned out to be, they would not get into trouble.

If the supervisor does supervise each of his inferiors one day in every three months (this would be a small hierarchy), he could hardly hope to know as much about any given inferior's scope of operations as that inferior did. Thus, even granting that the superior is both more intelligent and better informed about his own preferences than the inferior, he may frequently decide that the inferior is doing something wrong when the inferior's action is actually in accordance with the real interests of the man at the top.

If the supervisor enters a store in Tucson and observes that the brands of specialized Mexican food are a little peculiar, he does not know whether this indicates that the local manager is inefficient or that the customers have unique tastes. Furthermore, granted the short period of time that he can devote to the matter, he cannot hope to become well informed. It would take him more time to determine whether the assortment of Mexican-type food in the store is appropriate for the local customer assortment than it would take the local store manager who already has a great deal of background in that area. Thus, in a way, the supervisor is relatively inefficient in applying his time in judging what the inferior is doing.

Safeway does have an accounting system, and although it is not a perfect way of judging the efficiency of managers, it is a great help. Look at the government and consider what would happen if the attorney general decided to personally supervise the part of a local district attorney's decisions on whether to prosecute or accept a plea bargain.[2] The local attorney has a good idea of what local juries are like, knows the prejudices and characteristics of the local judges, and has talked to almost everyone concerned. He has a fair idea as to whether certain people will make good witnesses. Even if the attorney general is a better attorney than the local district attorney, the local district attorney's judgement would still be better than that of the attorney general unless the latter devoted considerable amounts of time to becoming thoroughly familiar with the case.

The point of all this is to re-emphasize that it is impossible for the higher supervisors to engage in detailed regulation of the lower-level people in a complex situation. The only way of obtaining any real control at these levels is to simplify the command structure by giving lower-level personnel more basic, routine tasks. Even then it is necessary to loosen the control operations considerably.

Returning to the accounting system, let us assume that the simple straightforward task given to lower-level officials is to maximize profits as shown in the accounts, and for the time being we will not discuss possible defects in those accounts. To ignore all of the difficulties faced by individual Safeway store managers, and to simply promote those with the highest profits and fire those with the lowest, is clearly not a perfect method of operation. It may, however, be close to the best we can do.

In practice, Safeway probably approximates that system because its lower-level supervisors know much more about the individual store than just its profit, and the higher-level supervisors have some confidence in their lower-level supervisors. Of course, that the lower-level supervisor with a division of, say, 20 stores is somewhat better supervised by simply looking at the profit ratio than the individual store manager would be because the law of large numbers comes to the aid of the higher-level supervisor.

In this case, also, the stock market, in simply looking at the total profit of each of a number of large diversified organizations, has an even better opportunity to make use of the law of large numbers. People who do best in the stock market have information about the companies in addition to knowing their profit ratios. Even here examination of the profit figures is not ideal, although a great many of the investors in the market use that simple system.

The situation with the government is more difficult. The old imperial Chinese government had a great advantage in that it was essentially a supervisory organization over a vast number of farming families with only small cities that were scattered evenly across the landscape. As mentioned earlier, they depended on individual examination-selected officials who were sent out to control what was their equivalent of a county without much in the way of central supervision. The central government knew if these officials were collecting their taxes and also knew whether there had been any riots or mob attacks in the area. Based on compliance with these two criteria, the government could fire is officials.

This system is not optimal, but a better alternative is hard to find, particularly because the man at the top in this case tended to be far from an ideal executive. He had been raised in the imperial palace under conditions that spoiled him; he had access to numerous forms of entertainment to distract his mind; and his intelligence was only average or even below average.

The officials who connected the magistrate running the county with the emperor were a chain of people who had passed the examination. Most had been county magistrates themselves at some point. Furthermore, the local governor would obviously know more about a given magistrate's performance than the emperor would and we have mentioned before the existence of the censor system checking on officials. As we said, the censorate rarely paid much attention to magistrates and normally concentrated on higher officials.

An advantage to this system is that it did economize on control and did not make an effort to push the central control to levels of detail that were not possible. The fact that the only central government official in most counties was the magistrate and the villages were actually self-governing was an even more striking illustration of the government's recognition of the declining marginal return on administration.

This system lasted for about 2000 years; in a way it is still retained by the Chinese communists. Their expectations have increased, however; they have more than one person in each county now, but they have retained the self-governing village though with less autonomy. They also have something roughly equivalent to the censorship in form of correspondence columns of their newspaper. People who write to the correspondence columns know that even if the paper doesn't publish their letter, someone will probably read it.

Although the system endured for a couple thousand years,[3] there were cyclical rises and falls of dynasties, catastrophic collapses of the whole government, invasions, famines, and floods. The system dealt with some issues well, others not; control over the imperial army was always difficult, whether that army was engaged in defending the Great Wall or carrying out punitive expeditions far north of there.

Having a number of people engage in similar tasks and then providing fairly lightweight supervision over them is characteristic of many government activities. The district attorneys are often appointed by the attorney general primarily for political reasons. The central government exercises relatively little control over them. If they have a reasonable level of success in court and if there are not too many public complaints about their deviation from the straight and narrow path, they will be left in. They are similar to the magistrates of the Chinese county except that they are district attorneys or specialized officials.

I mentioned earlier the impossibility of determining whether a given embassy is doing a good job, and, to give away a secret, the Department of State does not make any significant effort to find out. If all the routine steps are taken, the various reports filed at the right time, and congressmen pleasantly entertained, higher officials can expect a standard rate of promotion. In the lower ranks, improving your relations with those higher officials who fill out your efficiency report is more important than having good relations with the local government (of course, it may be necessary to have these good relationships in order to get a positive efficiency report).

Difficulties arise occasionally when something goes wrong. As ambassadors are shuffled from place to place, the secretary of state or his immediate inferiors could possibly cause a good deal of inconvenience for people at that rank, even though for political reasons they are reluctant to fire them.[4]

In this case, lower officers can be "selected out" by the personnel board. Most of them, however, are not, and most of them rise slowly to what we might call upper-middle rank with only a minority fortunate enough to go to the top. The key to promotion, as we have said earlier, is your relations to other people in the embassy, particularly your superiors — not what you are contributing to American foreign policy.

Both of these cases more or less follow the Chinese imperial pattern in relinquishing a large part of supervision and supervising only some tasks. In the case of the old empire and in the attorney general's case, what they are supervising is the most important aspect of the behavior of these lower officials. In the case of the Department of State that is not obvious, but since I have already conceded I can think of no way of supervising it efficiently, this is not said in a critical spirit.[5]

Relinquishment of the legislative role is another aspect of most democratic governments, particularly the federal government at the moment. U.S. congressmen sometimes complain bitterly that the President is not doing enough to get a particular piece of legislation through or has not provided them with a basic draft for legislation. While reducing their interests in legislation,[6] however, they have sharply increased their intervention in the executive branch. If you have a complaint about any branch of the federal government, the sensible thing to do is to call your congressman, especially if you are a recent campaign contributor, and you can expect attention from a staff member.

This is similar to the old Chinese system because the individual civil servant knows that there is not much detailed supervision of him from on high, but if he does something to trouble people of low rank, they will complain to their congressman. The congressman, depending on whether he thinks these people should be subject to trouble, will take action; hence, through this indirect way the official's behavior is supervised.

On the other hand, the local district attorney is less well informed about the desires of the attorney general than the attorney general is himself. In this case, there is no real way he can find out unless the attorney general tells him, and if the government really wants to have him duplicate the attorney general's preferences, the attorney general will probably have to spend a long time in what is for him the unfamiliar activity of laying out in detail exactly what his preference function is. Most people are not able to do so verbally.

Thus, the decision here made by the attorney general as a way of evaluating the district attorney is a difficult one, and the short cut of an accounting system simply does not exist. That he is in a worse situation than the division manager of Safeway should be obvious and not surprising.

But let us examine the actual difficulties here. The district attorney could rate his inferiors not in terms of examining one case but attempting to develop a sort of accounting procedure for them. He might, for example, count the number of cases they bring or the percentage of cases they win. Unfortunately, these two criteria are, to a considerable extent, in conflict with each other.

The district attorney who wants to win substantially all of his cases — and the federal district attorneys do win about 90 percent — can simply not bring difficult cases. One reason for the high crime rate in Manhattan was that for a number of years its state attorney did not like to lose cases. Therefore, his assistants did not bring cases unless they were reasonably sure they were going to win. Since the defense attorneys knew this, too, it meant that if you committed a crime in Manhattan under even moderately ambiguous circumstances, you did not risk punishment. Even if the evidence against you were quite strong, your attorney could probably talk the officiating assistant state's attorney into a favorable out-of-court settlement.

The state's attorney, at the time an elected official, could point out when the election came around that his conviction rate was high, which was true if conviction rate was taken as the number of convictions for cases brought. His conviction rate was low, however, if one took number of convictions for numbers of crimes.

An attorney who brings many cases out of a given universe of possible cases will have a high prosecution rate and a low conviction rate. The one who carefully selects only strong cases will have a high conviction rate and a low prosecution rate. The accounting method would have to measure both of these factors.

Designing a genuine suitable accounting rate would require further investigation of the complexities. There is a substantial large element of randomness in what particular crimes come to a given attorney. Hence, it would be necessary to use large samples if one is using some function of trial and conviction as a measure. Furthermore, attorneys in different areas would face various difficulties of this sort. In certain parts of Harlem, a white state's attorney would have great difficulty getting convictions, even if he were far more skilled, than his black compeer. This would, of course, indicate you should not appoint whites to the jobs in Harlem, but it also means that it is hard to compare the attorney in Harlem with the attorney out of Harlem.

The system of negotiating plea bargains makes this even more difficult because a state's attorney who is willing to accept relatively moderate pleas will, by that fact alone, get a higher conviction rate. A murderer who by agreement pleads guilty to breaking and entering[7] and goes up for one year counts as a conviction. If the district attorney is careful, no item may appear in the record indicating that he has been accused of murder.

All of these problems turn up with the Safeway manager although in a different structure. But for the Safeway manager, since the objective is fairly simple and straightforward and directly connected to his activities, that is, making a profit, his superiors have a way of measuring, at least to some degree of approximation, his contribution toward that objective.

I have chosen the case of the state's attorney as an example because we have a fairly clear idea of what we want him to do. We hope he would reduce the crime rate in his area by making committing crimes there dangerous and unpleasant, that is, sending people who commit crimes "up the river" for long periods. If he was successful, he would be dealing with fewer cases, although in the present-day world that is not likely to occur because he would probably not be that successful.

Other government activities indicate an even worse situation. For a lower-level official, one can tell more from a series of his accomplishments, rather than from an individual case, whether he tends to repeat the same methods as, for example, prosecuting attorneys do. But still, in many cases it is hard even to determine the outcome. The ambassador reports that he has had a successful conversation with the ministry of foreign affairs, with the result that he feels that the ministry will be more favorable to the United States in the future. It is almost impossible to tell if this is true.

Furthermore, suppose that relations between our country and another country deteriorate rapidly while under the aegis of a particular ambassador. It may reflect incompetence on the part of the ambassador, but it may also reflect his predecessor's incompetence, which is having a delayed effect; most likely, it reflects the international climate over which the ambassador has no control.[8]

In a similar group, it is frequently easier to judge the comparable abilities of higher-level officials than lower-level officials. An assistant state's attorney who is conducting trials will in the course of the year deal with only a somewhat restricted number of people. If the state's attorney office is large, however, and there are divisions in it, a division superintendent who had, say, ten state's attorneys under him, would have ten times that amount in his sample. Thus, the judgement of whether he is competent in running his branch of the service is easier to make than the question of whether the individual assistant state's attorney is doing a good job.

The same thing applies to Safeway. It is harder by just looking at the books to tell whether an individual store manager is doing a good job than it is for a division manager with, say, 20 stores under his control. The larger sample of data, which to some extent is random, is important.

As I mentioned previously, large profit-making companies also have individual divisions that are hard to evaluate. Suppose, for example, that our company has a corporate counsel who handles some of the cases personally and arranges for private counsel to handle others. Supervising his behavior is harder than supervising our state's attorney because of the fact the corporate counsel deals with so many different kinds of cases. He must make policy decisions about a range of issues: What shall we put on the label of a certain product? Should we produce a highly valuable and useful product cheaply that might lead to damage claims against the company at some future date? And so forth. Whether he is maximizing profits in these areas is clearly a very difficult problem, and the fact that we are now aiming at that simple objective, rather than the more complex set of objectives that we have in government, still does not make it easy.

So far, we have been talking about the supervisor allocating his time for supervision randomly but evenly across all his inferiors. There are two different methods of supervising inferiors: one involves accounting; the other, evaluating each case. The well-functioning supervisor will randomize his distribution of time between these two methods unless he is in the situation where one method dominates the other.

One technique, though not perfect, may help the supervisor to improve his supervision by giving up parts of his control. With this technique, the individual inferior has detailed policy instructions to carry out. The instructions themselves will not be optimal for all inferiors at all times, but their role in simplifying the supervision technique may more than compensate for individual nonoptimality.

In the case of Safeway, most things sold in the stores are provided through the Safeway warehouse and distribution system. Suppose that one manager discovers that, because of overbuying by the local wholesaler, he can get one type of canned goods much cheaper for this month than he could through the usual procedure. Will he be permitted to take that opportunity and advertise it locally as a bargain for shoppers? The question is not easy. Different chain stores follow different rules, but in general the manager would not be permitted to do so. The reason this profit opportunity is overlooked is because it makes supervision easier.

The point of this discussion has been to demonstrate that large organizations must be restricted. Perhaps some people will be surprised to hear this fact stated. It used to be true, and still is to some extent, that people of a socialist bent favored a planned economy — a central organization that gave everybody orders about everything except their consumption decisions. I remember being assured by an honor student at the University of Chicago Law School that by the socialist method we could double per capita incomes. He had just left the army, so this remark seemed particularly surprising. One would think that he would have observed that even a large and well-organized structure is not planned in detail from the center.[9]

Once we realize that this tight control is not possible, we have found another argument against the traditional planned economy and we have a higher degree of understanding of what organizations are. Indeed, adding a nail to the coffin of the planned economy is a work of supererogation in the present day. But if all of the other objections of planned economy were overcome, running a large hierarchical organization would be impossible.

In any large organization, officials control their own activities. Negotiations occur between different sub-bureaus. They even sign treaties with each other: for example, the famous "accord" under which the American government for a short period of time had a unified fiscal policy. Academic departments also frequently make deals with each other by trading, say, office space or time slots. Individual professors make deals with their department and with other professors. Profit-making institutions have a similar situation. The different subdivisions will disagree, hold formal negotiating sessions, and possibly enter into a contract with each other.

Members of any large organization always have a few tales to tell about their colleagues. One individual or one division is hard to get along with. They will also say that others are very cooperative. The fact that they are either cooperative or noncooperative, however, is a sure indication that somehow the orders coming from the top are not completely controlling things.

Those observations do not really contradict the existing literature, although in my opinion the literature puts too much emphasis on the degree to which the structure is internally coordinated and in the degree to which the orders go down from the top. But the dream once held by most proponents of the planned society is not held these days by any of the people who write on organizational theory.

This idealistic myth is sometimes still found in organization manuals or when introducing people to a particular organization. As I mentioned earlier, when I entered the Department of State I was given a tale of about how the low-level people collected information; how it was winnowed and partially integrated by the next stage and passed on up to the decision-making groups or individual who gave orders which were then passed down with each level elaborating on it so that it fit the various people at the bottom; from all this, the end product was a coordinated department with policy based on the best information. This was a myth, but I would not be surprised if the same myth is still being perpetrated in the Foreign Service Institute despite the probability that no one believes it.

If we cannot have this kind of perfect coordination, we should not try to establish organizations that require it to succeed. If we look around the world, we find that such organizations are avoided. Claims of perfect coordination are sometimes made, but no one actually acts on the hypothesis that they are true. We must cut our suit to fit our cloth.

Taylor, in pioneering the efficiency engineering profession, made one of his most important single discoveries when he realized that people could do more if less were asked of them. He adjusted shovel size to the weight of whatever was being thrown, which meant that people were using smaller shovels than they had before. In heavy work, Taylor frequently had people take a compulsory rest period every 15 minutes. Both of these reductions in the apparent size of the task actually increased daily productivity. We should do the same with our organizations.

An obvious case of reduced expectations is a corporation that is simply trying to make money and that uses an accounting system as a reasonably good way of telling whether inferiors are contributing to that goal. In addition, some direct supervision should be combined with that system.

This technique can be used only if your objective is making money. It is fortunate that our society is so organized that when a large number of people are attempting to make money, the wealth of other people will also be raised. Engineers who make minor improvements in automobiles do so in order to improve the profits of General Motors or Toyota, but I as a consumer benefit.

Unfortunately, there are many activities in which we cannot use this simple system. American cities, for example, do not provide incentives for homeowners to plant their gardens for an external coordinated appearance.

Most people are surprised at this possibility but if they look at cases in which a large area is all owned by one organization, say, a collection of apartment buildings with lawns and gardens around them, they will realize that centralized control does provide a more attractive environment. The feeling that large organizations such as the city government would not do as well, however, is, I think, justified.

Government or charitable activities comprise one large area in which we use centralized control without the use of cost accounting, since our objective is not to make profit. Some of these, like the post office, probably should be moved into the profit-making sector because competitive companies moving the mail, such as Federal Express and Purolator,[10] would do so more efficiently.

Air pollution, however, cannot apparently be dealt with in a similar way, although in that area many activities could be contracted out. The State of Arizona, for example, inspects all cars to find out whether their emission is dangerous from the pollution standpoint. They have just entered into a contract under which a private company will do this in return for a fixed fee. The cost will be lower than having the state do it, but here the company is carrying out a small and specified act concerned with pollution, not reducing air pollution in general. A solution for pollution can hardly be contracted out in this way.[11] Thus, the simple profit and loss statement of accounts cannot be used as a final determinant in this area although it may be used as an intermediate instrumentality.

In these areas we cannot expect even as much efficiency as we have in the market. There are, however, other reasons for undertaking these activities even if they are badly handled. The point is that we will continue to do some things that we want to do even if our implementation of them is quite wasteful.

To take a clearcut, straightforward example, suppose we have a dictator who has a strong set of preferences of some sort but is aware of the difficulties of bureaucratic control. To turn back to our attrition of control pyramid, the dictator will normally be able to impose his will on many more matters if he has a large bureaucracy than he can by himself. In a way, he is willing to let the acts of his bureaucracy for, say, 80 percent of their total volume, be things that he either does not know or care about if 20 percent are in accordance with his will. Hence, he has an increased impact on the environment. You may wish, as the dictator does, that the bureaucracy were more efficient than only implementing that 20 percent of the dictator's wishes, but nevertheless that is better than having them take all of their actions independently.

Napoleon, to take a good example of a dominating personality, certainly had only an approximate control of what his low-level officials were doing in various parts of Europe. Nevertheless, his will was carried out in Europe far better than it would have been had he not had this very large organization.

We can think of the matter from Napoleon's standpoint as follows. If he does not attempt to become emperor, he will be able to have almost all of his individual actions in perfect accord with his desires, but he will not have many people carrying out his instructions. If he becomes emperor and sets up a small organization with most local government decisions being determined by, say, local elected councils, he will have better control over that somewhat limited bureaucracy than he would have over a big bureaucracy. Nevertheless, the total number of actions undertaken by the governments which are in accord with his desires will be smaller than they would be if it were a single monolithic bureaucracy. However, a much higher percentage of those actions carried out by the small bureaucracy are in accord with his desires.

To use some numbers just for illustrative purposes, suppose that he establishes a small bureaucracy and is able to see that at least one-third of all actions undertaken by the lower-level members of the bureaucracy is in accordance with his desires. The total number of government actions taken in the society as a whole is 100,000 and this small bureaucracy deals with only 10,000 of them, with the others being dealt with by local bureaus. Thus, he has some 3,333 actions carried out in accord with his desires. If, on the other hand, he establishes a large all-encompassing bureaucracy, he is able to guarantee that the people at the bottom carry out his desires in only 10 percent of all the cases. But that is 10,000 cases instead of a little over 3,000.

Another technique would be to attempt to segregate government decisions so that the ones that Napoleon thought were most important were handled by a somewhat limited central bureaucracy and those he thought less important were handled by autonomous agencies. This course of action was actually carried out by Napoleon. In France, his word was law, although he made some pretense of having democratic agencies. Outside of France, he had a series of quasi-independent governments. Some of them were headed by his close relatives, but a number were headed by the traditional kings or emperors whom he had conquered in war. In this outer area, he certainly had great influence on the government, but he made no serious effort to control all its acts.

This system, no doubt, gave him a smaller total number of orders of his own implemented in the spirit in which they were given than if he had established one gigantic bureaucracy. On the other hand, it meant that a higher percentage of those orders were carried out in areas he thought were important. Deliberate abandonment of control in a number of areas thought to be less important permitted improved control in the narrower area that he thought was most important.

As I have pointed out, this particular technique is widely used. In a way, a corporation that gives local officials a high degree of autonomy, and then simply looks at the bookkeeping results, is one example. However, since the local authorities are ordered to "make profits", it is a bit different.

If we look at the world, this kind of decentralization or compartmentalization of orders is also widespread. I have already mentioned that the Chinese empire had a system in which the controls with respect to the gigantic local population were quite restricted, but in the areas where the emperor was concerned, he was able to get reasonably good compliance. This involved conscious delegating of power to locally elected village councils and magistrates of local counties. It also involved giving the lower-level officials a great deal of discretion. Again, control in less important areas was sacrificed in order to get better control in more important areas.

The Spanish empire at one point was the world's and Europe's largest empire.[12] It was governed largely by local officials. A local council controlled most of the affairs of its particular part of the empire, most of which would have little or no contact with a central structure. This council was normally appointed by higher level officials — a viceroy, for example — but it was also selected in terms of local popularity and influence. It was rather like the lord lieutenants in English counties who are officially appointed by the central government but are selected from a very narrow list of people who would be acceptable to the local community.

Although the federal systems of the United States and Switzerland seem to be other examples, when I discuss actual voters' control I will show that they are quite different. The central government is able to get its orders carried out in the army because it pays little or no attention to

street repair in Los Angeles. It has concentrated its orders to only part of
the system and left the other parts autonomous; hence, by relinquishing
its control in some areas, it attempts to control others.

The feudal systems in Europe and Japan, the only places where genuine feudalism existed, were other examples even though they were not
very successful. The higher officials, the kings, the emperors, and so on,
depended on the local officials, the earls, counts, and so on, almost exclusively for the provision of their armies. As we know, the provision of
the army was not very well done, but the original idea of giving the local
officials complete control over local affairs in return for their providing
military force, is not a priori foolish. Indeed, at the time that the idea was
instituted by the successors of Charlemagne, it may have been the best
option in a desperate situation.

To return to the somewhat more formal discussion, this particular technique involves the man at the top reducing his total bureaucracy by concentrating in areas that he thinks are most important. Most rulers have
done so whether they admit it or not. A leader can have two levels of
concentration of orders, or several. For example, during the early period
when Lenin ruled Russia, he was trying to set up a government that literally controlled everything. His attempt was a disastrous failure, and he
eventually recognized that he needed a "new economic policy". It is unfortunate for the poor Russians that his successors did not also realize
this need as well.

Although Lenin had a theoretically centrally controlled organization,
in practice, he did not attempt to deal with most activities. Local enterprises were put in control of the various people who were regarded as
respectable by the communist party and they were not given many orders
from the center simply because the center was busy with other matters.
The adopted principle of central control, therefore, was not able to be
practiced. The result was a set of enterprises and local governments being
run largely by autonomous groups. The central government concentrated
on political matters and a general policy.

One important matter was carefully controlled, however: the personal
security of Lenin and his immediate followers. They had as their guard
the Fourth Latvian Rifles, a special unit composed of non-Russians and
the only people in the whole of Russia at that time who were being paid
in gold.[13] Clearly, then, this security was a matter of high priority. I think
we can say that the system had several levels of control then, with the
highest exerted over their personal security guard, the second level over
political matters in connection with establishing their control, and the
third level, the actual control of the individual economic enterprises
which, in theory, was the system's whole objective.

In practice, this system worked badly, but not because of this compartmentalization. I above talked about systems in which there are two levels of control: for example, with Napoleon dealing quite personally with certain areas and leaving others to lower-level government agencies. In practice, many different degrees of control can be spread across the government, with some area subject to very close control, some with no control, and various intermediate stages for less important areas.

All this is efficient if we accept that control deteriorates as it goes down a large organization. That it deteriorates less rapidly in areas that you think are important and may not even exist in some areas is sensible. I will use another illustrative calculation — randomly fabricated — to clarify this point. Even if the numbers are not correct, the qualitative conclusions should be unchanged.

Suppose we have a society of 40 people, one of whom is a fairly dominating type with a good chance of becoming the dictator of an organization. Each of these 40 people in the average day performs 10 acts; these citizens, then, affect the outside world by 400 total acts each day.

One of them is the potential dictator, and under our present circumstances, 10 of the 400 acts are those he favors and the other 390 are randomly related to his desires. Suppose that he now becomes a complete authoritarian dictator using our previous three-for-one structure: i.e., he will have three immediate inferiors, each of whom supervises three, and each of them also supervises three. With this structure, there are now 27 people at the bottom having acts within the outside world, and the other 13 are our dictator and his supervisory personnel. The net effect is that there are 270 acts relating to the outside world, whereas before there were 400.

We will assume that at each stage there is a 25 percent deterioration, therefore, of the acts performed by the top-level inferiors who are simply supervising, 75 percent will be in accordance with the real wishes of the dictator and 25 percent not, and so on down the line. In this situation, the 27 people at the bottom will end up with 42.6 percent of their acts carrying out the wishes of the dictator, or a total of 113.90 acts.

On the other hand, 156.09 of their acts will not be in accordance with the dictator's preferences but will randomly distributed.[14] Certainly, from the dictator's standpoint, having roughly 114 acts in accordance with his desires in their effect on the outside world is better than 10. He has gained; in fact this is the largest number of acts affecting the outside world that he can have.

But let us suppose that there are some things he wishes to control in which his interests are more serious or more important than others. Assume that he establishes a smaller organization for the purpose of dealing with fewer things — specifically, one organization in which he has three supervisors under his control and they each control three people who actually affect the outside world. In other words, we drop off the bottom rank. In this case, there will be 270 acts that are not controlled because they are performed by people who are not part of the hierarchy, 90 acts performed by the bottom nine people in the hierarchy, so, again, the total number of acts performed is less than the original 400, and not all of those bottom 90 acts are in accordance with the desires of the dictator. Using our 25 percent deterioration, we find that 56 percent of the acts at the bottom level are performed in accordance with the desires of the dictator, or 50 together. The people at the bottom also perform 39.6 acts that are not in accordance with his desires, and the total number of acts thus is therefore 309.6.

Obviously, this situation is less desirable from the standpoint of the dictator unless the 50 acts that are now subject to control are more important than the others. There is no reason why that could not be so and, as a matter of fact, most dictators do follow this kind of a pattern or some system under which they have even less control. In other words, the dictator has reduced his total control over the environment in order to concentrate his control over some things that he finds very important.

Our final model here is one in which the dictator has not two but three levels of importance for acts. The things he thinks are important, he does himself; we will assume he uses one-third of his time and therefore gets 3.3 contacts with the outside world perfectly in accord with his preferences. There is another one-third of the acts which are dealt with through a very small bureaucracy. Since he is now devoting one-third of his time to controlling that bureaucracy, he does not get 50 contacts with the outside world in accordance with his preferences, but only 20. The rest of the society is also organized in a gigantic hierarchy with him at the top, and he devotes only one-third of his time to supervising that, with the result that 20 of their acts are not in accordance wit his preferences. For a grand total, he has 43.3 acts in accordance with his preferences.

Clearly, this situation is worse than either of the other two, but he has stratified things so that the most important acts are certainly in his control, the second level of importance are to a considerable extent under his control, and the ones that are least important are only modestly controlled. Whether this is better than the earlier systems depends on whether he has strong feelings about which policies are most important.

This fabricated structure is actually quite realistic. Supervisors, whether they are dictators or branch managers of Safeway, do make some decisions themselves for direct action to the outside world; they supervise some through a narrow hierarchy; they allow many aspects to be dealt with by a wide hierarchy. Even this system with three levels of importance is a simplification since many things are seen as not significant enough to supervise.

We began this chapter with a discussion of the difficulties of getting perfect control, and then we proceeded to a way of organizing a bureaucratic structure so that the man or group at the top abandons some part of that control in order to get more important desires fulfilled and tasks accomplished. This dictatorial model could be replaced by a democratic model with the voters at the top. In the next chapter we will look into other ways of reducing the total span of control.

Notes

1. Which they did still when I was in the infantry in World War II.

2. This actually means how stiff he will be in his plea bargaining negotiations. The actual terms are what determines whether it will go to trial.

3. The examination system was actually only about 1000 years old but various methods of selecting people for much the same characteristics were in use before that.

4. It is possible to fire an American ambassador even if he is a career officer, though it is difficult.

5. In a way, I do criticize the Department of State — not for the way it is internally run but for its size. Granted the impossibility of controlling it better than it is now we could get by with somewhere about 1 percent as many people overseas as we now have.

6. This does not mean that the total amount of legislation has been reduced. It is just that it is not read by the congressmen.

7. As part of his murder.

8. Grew, one of our best diplomats, was ambassador to Japan in the thirties. Our bad relations with them surely cannot be blamed on him. For a reverse case, our (politically appointed) ambassador in London during much of World War II was literally inarticulate. Our relations with England were nevertheless excellent.

9. This was right after World War II, and the anti-military prejudice of modern intellectuals was not much in evidence at that time. Most of my classmates were proud of their own service in the military and of the American military machine, although all of them had tales of bureaucratic bungle.

10. When I was a boy, Purolator was a specialized company that took care of water softeners in parts of the United States where the limestone problem was serious.

11. Research about it could be contracted out.

12. It outreached the later English empire since it included both North and South America, and extensive holdings in both Africa and Asia. To give one piece of history that is normally overlooked in American textbooks, Philip, for a period of time, was married to the Queen of England. Although he was not formally recognized as king, this probably made little or no difference, and he lived in London. The disintegration of this vast empire in the 17th century rather than its power in the 16th century, dominates our history books.

13. Lenin had set up a small secret treasury of diamonds which was for the purpose of providing support for the leaders of the government if it was necessary for them to flee abroad. Perhaps that could be regarded as being a real security system as well as the gold payments to the Fourth Latvian Rifles.

14. In this example, I am assuming for the sake of simplicity that the act that each person has has many different possibilities so that the prospect of an individual just accidentally doing what the dictator wants is substantially zero.

10 RENT SEEKING AND THE IMPORTANCE OF DISORGANIZATION

Currently, rent seeking is all the rage in economics. Since I actually invented the idea, although not the name, the reader might be surprised if I did not discuss it in this book.[1] That is not the only reason for bringing it up. One aspect of rent seeking is of great importance in the internal structure of any large organization.

A number of organizations engage in rent seeking with the intent of improving their absolute size. For example, some corporations have lobbyists in Washington to ensure that tariffs protect them from foreign competition. Farm organizations also exist whose primary purpose is raising farm prices.

Rent seeking is the activity of attempting to get some kind of special advantage from society that benefits you but actually injures other people. Organizing a monopoly would be a case in point. In the present day, it would more likely be accomplished through pressure and lobbying the government than by the mainly private methods once used by J.P. Morgan.

There are many other ways of getting these special advantages. The Central Arizona Project is not a monopoly, it is a highly wasteful system of canals and pumps that provides water to a select group of beneficiaries at a cost to the taxpayer which is vastly higher than its actual value. Nevertheless, it was obtained by rent seeking.

The man who invents something of value, patents it, and then sells it for profit has achieved a rent, but we don't call this rent seeking. He has obtained his profit by doing something that benefits society, and in a competitive market it is difficult to obtain a profit by measures that do not benefit other people. The man who has not invented anything new, but gets the government to restrict his competitors, on the other hand, is engaged in rent seeking.

The market is not a zero-sum game. Some activities produce a profit and some cause a loss. The individuals who participate in the profitable activities are not regarded as rent seeking, while those getting a profit for themselves while lowering the gross national product (GNP) are rent seeking.

Most of the new work in rent seeking is an effort to deal with the additional costs caused by this activity. From the first article[2] I wrote, the main theme has been that the higher cost to society from these activities — much higher than economists previously thought. Anne Krueger, in an important article,[3] estimated that the cost of this kind of rent seeking from one type of situation alone, foreign exchange certificates, was 7 percent of the GNP of India and 15 percent in Turkey. Those are big figures, particularly with the high number of rent seeking activities in both countries.

Many experts on the Orient believe that the basic reason for much poverty in China and India despite their ancient and highly developed civilizations, is the dominance of rent seeking as the principal form of economic activity by the more aggressive segments of their population. Fortunately, the United States has not experienced this activity as intensely.

But the point of this discussion is not organization of the company in order to generate rents from dealing with the government or its customers. Although that would be efficient from the corporation's point of view, we hope that the corporation won't be efficient along those lines. That would compare to drug dealers also being efficient in their business.

What we are concerned about is rent seeking in the interior of the corporation. Let us elaborate on our previous discussion of leverage buyouts.[4] Suppose that we have a large corporation, and there appear to be profits from taking it over and reorganizing it. The method of taking it over has changed over time. Long ago it was proxy fights, then it became the activities of corporate raiders, and now it tends to be leveraged buyouts. Let us consider the typical leverage buyout of a mythical Behemoth Corporation.

Senior executives of Behemoth get in contact with a banker willing to bankroll them and offer to buy the entire common stock of the company at a price that typically is about 50 percent above the market value before people heard about the leverage buyout effort. Let's assume that they are successful.

The new management, which is the old management who now owns the corporation instead of being paid employees, needs to sell off a number of subsidiaries and use the money to repay part of the gigantic loans they have received. Because of the size of the loans, however, the bankers charge a somewhat higher interest rate than they would for an ordinary loan. It's rather surprising how little the premium and interest rate are in these cases, but it is positive.

The common stockholders who sold their stock have obviously made a large profit — about 50 percent of the previous value of their stock. There is no particular prediction here about the people who buy the segments the company sold off. Presumably they were sold off at a reasonable price and the purchasers on the whole do reasonably well. If they did wonderfully well, it would imply that the new management sold the segments too cheaply.

The operation itself, however, in most cases turns out to be modestly — not immensely — successful. It now has a very much larger capital value, most of which is denominated in debt, and hence must make a larger return on its assets to pay interest on that amount and still retain a reasonable profit. Normally it is able to obtain as good returns on this enlarged "capital" as the original corporation did on the earlier "capital". It does not usually make extraordinarily high returns as a percentage of the new "capital".

The new management is subject to considerably more pressure for efficiency because it now holds only a highly leveraged part of the corporation, and minor slippage in efficiency can wipe them out. They perhaps have an equity which is $150 million and have bonds outstanding of $1,350 million. These bonds pay a relatively high rate of interest. Before the buyout the stockholders had an equity worth $500 million with bonds in the amount of another $500 million.

How does this new management succeed? They are the same people who were running the corporation before, but they now must be making a much larger return on the same body of physical assets. Of course, they have sold off some of these physical assets to repay part of the debt. But they now have a much higher bonded indebtedness for the assets that they retained.

The answer seems to be twofold. One is that these managers, themselves being subject to much stronger pressure, simply work harder. The other is that the only major changes we always observe in such cases is a large-scale purge of the middle management. Many people in what I've referred to as "the corporate swamp" are fired. These two changes observed in all of these corporations[5]seem to be enough.

These corporations now proceed to produce a considerably higher return on their physical assets than they did before; indeed they have to if the corporation is to remain out of bankruptcy. Why would this elimination of people who previously were voluntarily hired by substantially the same management greatly increase efficiency? That it does increase efficiency, I think, is fairly clear because once again these companies are able to survive and pay the interest on their bonds in most cases, although their current bonded indebtedness is very much higher than the sum of the bonded indebtedness and equity was before.

To explain this, we must turn to an internal version of rent seeking. Ronald MacKean, when explaining a difference between private companies and nonprofit or government agencies, used to say that in a private company, if the owner saves money he can take it home with him. In a nonprofit or a government agency, he can't.

The reason MacKean thought this was important was essentially psychological. Many unpleasant decisions must be made if you want to maximize profits. You have to fire people you personally like, you have to put pressure on your inferiors even though this clearly will mean that your relations disintegrate, you may have severe fights with, let us say, your labor union or with neighboring organizations who are competing with you, even though in the case of the nonprofit and government, the word *competition* is not always used.

Furthermore, all of these basically unpleasant decisions must normally be made rather quickly, before you have obtained enough information so that you're certain. Doctors talk about difficult decisions in medical strategy. For example,[6] it used to be said that a doctor had to make certain strategic decisions when it came to cutting off people's legs. A doctor who was a radical and cut off many legs would cut off legs that did not need it. A doctor who was conservative and who rarely cut off legs would not have that problem, but he would have patients die who otherwise wouldn't.

The same type of dilemma confronts most managers. The decision to fire someone or simply yell at him, all of which tend to reduce the pleasantness of your environment, can best be made before the evidence is completely in. If you wait until it all is in, you will find that your competitors have beaten you out. Thus, you will almost certainly make mistakes which are likely to be brought firmly to your attention — which makes life even more unpleasant.

For the owner of a company, the pain is compensated by the fact that he can take the money home with him after he has made the decision, even if he chooses to take some kind of risk. It's his money he's risking, and whether this will make him be more cautious or less cautious depends on his personality. But if he is a hired employee of a company and he does something that is risky but has high profit potential, if the profit potential is achieved he will receive back only a small part of it. If, on the other hand, the company is driven into bankruptcy, he will suffer a large loss.

A relatively risk neutral person would probably be more likely to take chances with his own corporation than with a corporation by which he is hired. I have a friend who, for a time. was a high official in one of the more powerful and older American corporations. He said one of the real functions of the committee structure in this corporation was that it permitted people to take large risks without any responsibility. You never could trace any losses back to anyone. This protection may have offset the other phenomena.

This is the difference between the owner of a corporation and an employee of a government or nonprofit organization. Think of the higher ranking employees of a large corporation. They face somewhat the same kind of problem, though not as extreme. They are not going to take home the entire profit of the company nor will they pay the full cost if it loses. On the other hand, they will pay the full cost in their personal relations — the need to fire people they like and admire, the need to face rumors floating around about how he fired so-and-so because the man resented his attentions to his wife, and so forth, and in addition he only gets part of the return.

Another issue important here is a little way down the pyramid rather than at the absolute top: the development of minor tradeoffs and alliances. People who saw that wonderful movie, *9 to 5* will recall that there was one unsympathetic character who is listed as a "spy for the boss". She passes along to higher officials things that the lower officials don't want them to get. One understands perfectly why other people didn't like her, but from the standpoint of the efficiency of our total economy or that corporation only, she was performing a social function. When the other people succeeded in sending her off to Paris to prevent her from reporting a fairly major sin to their superiors, they were lowering efficiency.[7]

Anybody who's been in an organization knows about efforts to prevent information which would be of use to higher officials from getting to them. For example, I was in a rather small organization in which one of the secretaries characteristically arrived late. It did not affect her getting the work done; she was indeed very efficient. Nevertheless, the office supervisor reported her to the head of the organization. The other secretaries regarded this as a crime almost equivalent to rape.

Normally, the situation is not as clearcut as in that incident. Almost everybody around the office participates in a certain amount of relaxation, and all of them refrain from reporting it because they worry about reciprocation. There is a sort of bargain whereby you don't cause trouble with the superiors for me and I won't cause it for you. This is rent-seeking that reduces not only the profits of the company but the GNP.

In addition to this kind of bargaining, over time if people are operating in the same office in close contact, many personal relation will develop — mostly friendship, but antagonism, too. Friendship also leads to people's not reporting.[8] Of course, rivalry and intense chronic infighting between colleagues occur just as commonly as covering up defects.

But even this rivalry may mean that defects are covered up. Most people who are fighting their way to the top are attempting to cultivate relations with certain superiors and develop a train of inferiors behind them. Therefore, they have strong motives to protect some people while knifing other people in the back. Again, information may not go upward.

The higher officials who live in an environment with a certain amount of ambiguity will, if they press hard, get more efficiency out of their inferiors than if they don't press, but they also have less in the way of pleasant relationships. This is because they don't take the funds home. Here is the reason for the basic improvement in efficiency with these leverage buyouts. The higher officials can take the money home with them. Indeed, they're in a situation where if they do not improve efficiency, they might lose the money they've already put in and go through bankruptcy. Under the circumstances, their environment changes rapidly and their behavior changes in an equally radical way. Suddenly they may begin to work harder themselves in addition to putting pressure on their inferiors and firing people in large numbers. Apparently the "corporate swamp" described earlier shrinks by about a third.

The total cost saving in firing this one-third of middle managers is not very great although it is worth picking up. These middle managers face a change in the incentive structure when they suddenly realize that their superiors are no longer likely to be tolerant and understanding. The money these superiors can make by putting screws on a particular junior manager is now preferable to pleasant relations with him.

The people running corporations have dealt with this problem by instituting various bonus schemes. The leverage buyout is really a large bonus scheme as well as a severe increase in pressure on the people concerned. That it pays off is fairly good evidence that a lot of administrative slack and rent-seeking exists even in well-managed private corporations. Compared to what there is in nonprofits and the government, of course, it is trivial. Still, here we have a case of internal rent seeking.

Another instance can be found in governments who frequently shift military officers around. They justify it as training. The actual reason, however, is I think much more ancient. Shifting people around makes it much harder for them to develop the kind of personal relations with each other which might make the military dangerous.[9]

Obviously, the operators of a large corporation don't need to worry about this problem. A low-ranking official may indeed engage in intrigue and succeed in replacing the current chairman of the board, but he does so by attracting the favor of the stockholders and other directors and not by literally overthrowing him. He does not necessarily need the active assistance of, say, a majority of the officials, so it differs as such from a military coup.

Large corporations shift their junior managerial personnel around a great deal. Furthermore, these shifts are commonly geographical, which is a great inconvenience for most junior officials. Surely corporations have to pay these officials higher salaries than if they didn't impose these transfers on them.

This approach is clearly an effort to make the kind of quiet interoffice trades that you don't talk about me and I won't talk about you more or less impossible. Because nobody has deep personal ties with anyone else, there is less rent-seeking behavior. Furthermore, if an individual does something to irritate one of his colleagues, the cost is modest because either he or the colleague will be going somewhere else shortly. Thus this shifting, although apparently inefficient in that it prevents specialization and requires higher wages, is actually quite efficient.

Roger Congleton has pointed out that the committee itself may, in a special way, reduce rent seeking activity.[10] Personal goals are harder to push through a committee than through an individual because of the number of people to convince. An offsetting factor is that individuals do not have as much riding on the matter and therefore may put less energy into it. Nevertheless, there surely is some truth in Congleton's position. It would indicate that the innumerable committees, which we observe in large corporations and meetings on all sorts of subjects, actually serve the function of making rent seeking somewhat less severe.

Also, although one must keep good relations with one's colleagues, there is something to be gained by stabbing one of them in the back. Complex and devious intrigues must frequently be concealed not only from their superiors but from many of their equals and inferiors, which makes it harder for these intrigues to be implemented.

The net effect is that certain types of rent seeking are reduced by the structure. The corporate swamp, in addition to having the characteristics we have discussed before, also makes it harder to carry off various rent seeking activities than a simpler command structure.

This means not that individuals are pressed to be highly efficient, but that it's rather dangerous for them to engage in more rent seeking than is the norm. There may be a gradual fall in the energy with which they push the objectives of the corporation. The tendency to avoid unpleasant clashes with their colleagues, and so on, can grow. As long as it is general, it will not lead to career difficulties. The standard by which officials are judged gradually falls, with resulting inefficiency.

This is the reason that the sharp increase in pressure which we have described in the takeovers tends to be efficient. The average level of work intensity and devotion to the corporate ideals can gradually slide down in the bureaucracy and the buyout brings it up again to a high level. It's dangerous to be lazier, more devious and plotting, and more interested in internal matters within the company than the average official in your office. It's not dangerous to stick with the average level even if it is going steadily downward.

These are private corporations. How about government agencies? The first thing to be said is that although the military followed the rotation system I have described, as do the Department of State and the FBI, many other government agencies do not.

Although this shifting around does reduce the speed with which the net efficiency of the organization declines, it doesn't reduce it to zero. We can say that the FBI is more efficient than the Post Office, but obviously this is not strong praise.

The efficiency of the government is even further reduced by the fact that, in practice, it's very very difficult to fire anyone. It's also difficult to demote them; even denying them routine promotion is hard. Libecap's studies[11] show that the principal characteristic of promotion is simply seniority.

Under these circumstances we would anticipate a great deal of rent seeking in which people simply don't work very hard, are not devoted to the objectives of their organization, and so on. We can also anticipate that if they are interested in some aspect of their agency — for example, expanding it — they could freely devote a lot of energy to it. We would expect the average efficiency to be lower with no prospect of a true takeover bid dealing with it.

The absence of the takeover bid was once not that important in the United States or in other democracies. The election in part served that purpose. The bulk of the government employees could be fired at any time, and when a new government came in, it had a strong tendency to purge the existing structure. The politicians, although they did want the roads to be properly repaired, had other things they wanted the civil servants to do as well. They seem to have paid the civil servants more than the going rate while requiring them to pay the surplus in campaign contributions to the party in power. Nevertheless, there was something like the takeover bid. In those days the government was smaller, and the votes of its employees weren't especially important.

All this has changed. Civil servants today are almost guaranteed against being fired and hence the bulk of them do not make campaign contributions. Indeed, it's actually illegal for them to do so although there are various indirect ways to circumvent it. More important, their numbers and votes have increased greatly. As a result we now have a situation in which the politicians cannot fire the civil servants but the civil servants, if the politicians do something that actually annoys them, can fire the politicians. This has led to a further decline in net efficiency.

Here's a true horror story. A political appointee in the Reagan administration discovered that one of his high-ranking civil servants was never in the office. When he inquired, learned that the man was a dipsomaniac and was home drunk. Since the appointee had some crusading fervor, he decided that the civil servant should be fired if he did not cure himself.

The lengthy procedure for getting rid of a civil servant requires that his supervisor have several interviews with him in which the defects of his work are pointed out. Since the man was almost never in the office this approach proved difficult. However, when it was finally accomplished, the man was fired. He promptly sued the government for reinstatement, and the Civil Service Commission not only reinstated him, but compelled the government to pay his lawyer's fee.

The Civil Service Commission regards as its principal activity the protection of people from their political superiors. A great deal of political clout lies behind this protection because there are so many civil servant votes. The civil servants don't have very much in the way of positive ideas when they vote, but the politician who chooses to take them on is going to find himself out of office before he gets rid of very many of them.

The net result of this is another example of the kind of rent seeking which we have been describing inside the corporation, but immensely more powerful. Friendly relations with colleagues, complicated intrigues about matters which in general are of no great importance, and rivalry with other parts of the government are all what we would expect and what we get. We observe this in local, state, and federal government but it is much more severe in the federal government than in the other levels. This is partly because there are more civil servants in the national government, but also because of the great distance between the average civil servant and the voters.

In local governments, for example, many potential increases in funds available for government activities actually require a popular vote either for a bond issue or a tax increase. It does you little good as a civil servant to vote against the mayor of your city if his replacement is still unable to increase taxes and use the money to raise your salary. But this is unfortunately not true of the federal government.

One of the results of all this is a move to amend the constitutions of many states to require balanced budgets and let various particular expenditures be put to popular vote. As Bennett and DiLorenzo have proved in their *Underground Government*[12] these limitations have by no means been completely successful, but they undoubtedly make the lives of various bureaucrats more difficult than they otherwise would be.

Currently there is a movement afoot in the state governments to put restrictions on the length of time that a legislator can serve. In California, it is a constitutional amendment. It makes this kind of rent seeking more difficult, thus perpetrating the present situation in which local government is more efficient.

One offsetting problem is that the individual legislators will all be less experienced in dealing with their jobs. Whether this is important is a matter left to the reader.

Let us return to the title of this chapter, "Rent Seeking and the Importance of Disorganization". When an organization gets more thoroughly acclimated to its task and develops a greater degree of specialization, two things happen. First, all its employees accumulate more knowledge of their task and hence have a greater ability to carry it out. Second, they acquire more knowledge of what they can get away with, who their true friends are — who should be protected and who will protect them — and what the best rent seeking method is of getting promoted or getting other advantages. One of these two improves the efficiency of the corporation, and the other reduces it. The only known way of eliminating the second is to impose some kind of disorganization on the corporation that may take the form of a leverage buyout or simply the transfer of personnel from one place to another.

Obviously we have a tradeoff here. The company or government that shifted all its personnel around every day would never get anything done. On the other hand, the company or corporation that leaves its personnel in the same position has a group of highly skilled individuals with their skills emphasizing rent seeking and avoiding work.

The rotation of personnel is one way of laying off this tradeoff with the appropriate time in job, varying from job to job from one company and government organization to another. This system, per se, however, is not really sufficient. General corporate culture can withstand rotation and corporate culture can lead to a gradual relaxation and lowering of standards. This means that more drastic reorganizations are necessary from time to time.

The private market takes care of this by such things as bankruptcy, corporate reorganizations imposed by the creditors or by new stockholders, the leverage buyout, and so on. Governments have little opportunity for doing so, particularly in the present circumstances where the bulk of their employees can't be fired almost regardless of what they do.

The standard Chinese historic theory about the rise and fall of dynasties has as one of its arguments the gradual growth and corruption of the bureaucracy. Granted that the Chinese bureaucrats were all selected by a difficult examination and were automatically moved every five years or more frequently; clearly this extends past the interoffice friendship problem. A gradual relaxation of the corporate culture is what eventually leads to a new dynasty after the old one collapses.

If we look back over history, we see that democracies have never been permanent organizations. We must work out some equivalent of the type of periodic sharp disorganization that is vital to the maintenance of the efficiency of private corporations.

This chapter has been devoted to rent seeking within large corporations and government. Keeping it under control is a problem, one which the corporations have handled much better than the government. It should be remembered that this is internal rent seeking. Corporations frequently are engaging in the other kind of rent seeking — efforts to get monopolies or special privilege out of the government — and the more efficient they are in repressing their internal rent seeking, the more likely they are to be efficient in getting these rent seeking special privileges.

Notes

1. My original article was "The Welfare Costs of Monopolies, Tariffs and Theft" but further work has been done by all sorts of people. This has been collected in *Toward the Theory of the Rent Seeking Society* edited by James Buchanan, Robert Tollison and Gordon Tullock, (College Station: Texas A & M Press, 1980) and *The Political Economy of Rent Seeking* edited by Charles Rowley, Robert Tollison and Gordon Tullock (Boston: Kluwer Academic Publishers, 1988). I have done a book of my own called *Economics of Special Privilege and Rent Seeking* (Boston: Kluwer Academic Publishers, 1989).

2. "The Welfare Effects of Monopolies, Tariffs, and Theft", *op. cit.*

3. Krueger, Anne O. "The Political Economy of the Rent-Seeking Society", *American Economic Review* 64 (June 1974), 291–303.

4. An excellent summary of recent work in this area is contained in Andrei Shleifer and Robert W. Vishny, "The Takeover Wave of the 1980s," *Science* (17 Aug. 1990), 745–749.

5. It is now more highly specialized because it has sold off some of its subsidiaries.

6. This is before the antibiotics which have made these problems much easier.

7. In this particular case that was not true. Complex and indirect results of getting rid of her did indeed raise the profits of the company. This would not happen very often in the real world.

8. The corporation I used to work for had a rule against hiring husband and wife pairs. It was thought this kind of interrelation led to personnel difficulties.

9. The English have gone at this in a somewhat different way. If you join the British Army as either an officer or an enlisted man, you join a particular regiment and you stay in that regiment until you either die, resign, or are promoted to general officer. Furthermore, the regiments are trained in such a way that they have a great deal of regimental patriotism and tend to look down on all the other regiments. Conspiracy among them is almost impossible.

10. Congleton, Roger D. "Committees and Rent-Seeking Effort," in *Journal of Public Economics* 25, (1984), 197–209.

11. Libecap, Gary D. and Johnson, Ronald N. "Bureaucratic Rules, Supervisor Behavior, and the Effect on Salaries in the Federal Government," in *Journal of Law, Economics, and Organization* V (Spring 1989) 53–82.

12. Bennett, James D. and DiLorenzo, Thomas J. *Underground Government,* (Washington D.C.: CATO Institute, 1982).

11 RESTRICTED SCOPE

Chapter 9 ended with a discussion of ways in which the dictator or person in control of some area could improve his actual control of the world by reducing the number of things he attempts to control and/or by giving different levels of control to different things depending his perceptions of their importance. After the digression to internal rent seeking in Chapter 10, we will continue with our discussion of control in this chapter and, in fact, will become more radical.

To begin with, in Chapter 9, I pointed out the possibility of confining your direction to only a few inferiors or giving different levels of direction to different inferiors. There is another way of doing the same thing that can change the level of supervision: you give to your inferiors different degrees of intensity of supervision by subject matter. For example, the division manager of Safeway might make it a habit to visit all his stores at about the same frequency, but while in the store he might look carefully at the meat counter and ignore the detergent section.

This approach would involve a differential investment of resources, but it could also simply recognize reality. Let us suppose that it is easy to tell whether a supermarket has given the right amount of shelf space for different brands of detergent, but that determining whether the meat assortment is proper is much more difficult. The same level of control could be attained by different investments of time in these two areas.

On the other hand, there might be a difference of importance in addition to the difference in difficulty of control. Assume, for example, that to get an idea of the degree to which a meat display is done properly takes about three times as much time as for the same inspection of the detergents. If, on the other hand, you felt that the meat area was much more important, you might nevertheless give it five times as much time as the detergents. This, again, could improve efficiency.

There might be other aspects of the inspection process to which the supervisor would not need to give any conscious attention at all. The external appearance of the store and whether the aisles are clean would be matters which I presume he would not consciously consider but nevertheless would notice if something were wrong. I do not know whether this should be listed as supervision. Perhaps the inspector would spend more time walking through the store than just taking the most direct route from his entry to the place he wants to inspect in order to allow himself the opportunity to notice something like this, but more likely it would be a pure byproduct.

The combination of giving different amounts of time to different inferiors and different amounts of time to different aspects of the inferiors' work would be optimally efficient and, again, would mean that the number of things were done which were not in accord with the preferences of the superior, but this would be a byproduct of getting performance more in accordance with his preferences in certain areas.

Again there is the problem here of not permitting your inferiors to know too much of what you are doing. The supervisor may normally, upon entering the store, look at the meat counter very carefully and only glance briefly at the detergent shelves. It would be sensible, however, for his inferiors to know that once in a while he looked carefully at the detergent shelves. He wants his inferiors to devote more attention to the meat shelves than to the detergent shelves, but he does not want them to ignore the detergent shelves totally.

Although a random pattern is desirable, in this case the general pattern of the randomization should be known by the inferiors. They should not be able to predict when he enters the store what he will look at, but they have a weighting function that tells them the probability that he will look at different things. This gives him optimal supervision efficiency.

The main theme of this chapter is that the individual who wants to be effective must confine himself to a fairly restricted area. He must accept that his work will have limited scope simply because he has human limits.

At the time of this writing, the communist societies in Eastern Europe are in a state of at least temporary disintegration. As the disintegration proceeds, it becomes more obvious that they had not succeeded in their original goal of controlling everything. The higher level was issuing orders, but the lower levels were not obeying them. In fact, it seems likely that the Tolkach and the black market were the basic coordinating factors in their economy.

Certain orders were carried out. For example, one that guaranteed that no one could be fired no matter how inefficient he was apparently had a great deal of public support. Other orders — ones that told individuals to introduce new equipment, invent, and so on — were carried out in a restricted way. They copied foreign developments with a lag. Russia is in the process of getting into the stage that Italy had reached, say, in 1950, when traffic jams were just starting to be common; the number of cars is exceeding the capacity of the streets.

The quality of their goods is known to be poor. It is unfashionable to wear Russian clothes if you can possibly get Western clothes. New technology is confined almost exclusively to the military. Even so, for example, the atom bomb was undoubtedly stolen from the United States, although perhaps not the hydrogen bomb. In the case of the atom bomb, the permeable barriers of their separation device were made in East Germany because the Russian plants could not meet the manufacturing specification, and all this at a time when they were vigorously accusing the United States of developing a nuclear arms industry in Germany.

Two different industrial sectors apparently exist in Russia, one concerned with arms which does a reasonable job, and the other concerned with everything else. In essence, it would appear that the higher-ranking Russians concentrated their attention strongly on things that were reflected directly in their living standard.[1]

The second priority should have been the security apparatus, but it would appear that everyone except Castro and Ceausescu felt confident enough so that they did not devote much attention to this part of the organization. Policemen, army officers, and even to some extent the special political police have turned out to be quite unreliable in Eastern Europe, and in Russia they do not seem to be playing any role in the current difficulties.[2]

A third level of priority would appear to be control over the military which at the higher level the party certainly retained. The economy itself came in as a fourth level. Even in this fourth level, they seem to have tried to control only portions of the economy and were apparently perfectly happy to have the black market continue functioning without much concealment.

There were elaborate plans, but the plans were normally based on inadequate information, and the lower officials had strong motives to deceive. No one paid much attention to failures of those plans in anything except the most obvious way. Indeed, the plans frequently led to severe distortion. Under an agreement with Fiat, the old Fiat car equipment was all shipped to Russia and a plant was set up to produce the old small Fiat while Fiat itself moved on to higher and better things. After some time, it was decided to try and export some cars to the West. This led to a number of difficulties, including the British motoring association refusing to drive the car from dock to their test area on the grounds that it was intrinsically too dangerous.[3]

All of this is not to criticize the Russian government. Although as I suppose the reader knows, I detested it. Under the circumstances they were recognizing the real requirements of their job. It was not possible for them to carry out the official theory of their society. What they did, in addition to seeing that they themselves lived fairly well, was to provide a superficial appearance that a plan was being carried out while permitting various things to go on that were not in accordance with it.

The superficial appearance seems to have fooled most of Western intellectuals, and more important, a number of Russians, even the ones who themselves regularly used the black market.

The problem here, or the solution, appears to lie in Plato's distinction between the "essence" and the "accidents". Everyone believed that the essence of the Russian system was planning and so forth. But there were the accidents, the difficulties of the real world which were thought of as deviations from a great grand plan which was the essence of the system. In fact, it seems likely that the "deviations" were the essence of the system and the grand plan was purely decorative.

Having a purely decorative plan is not at all uncommon. Many American companies occasionally have drawn up a program for the future, and since expensive executives devote some time to making them up, we must assume that they perform some function. Whatever the function is, however, it is not to control the future in any detail.

Such plans are omnipresent. My sister and brother-in-law live in a small town in Iowa, and the town has just received, courtesy of the federal taxpayer and the University of Northern Iowa, a plan for the next 12 years. It is a nice plan and its authors, experienced in such matters, make parts of it vague enough so as not to be caught out by actual developments. But it would be mere coincidence if the city actually carried out the plan.

The reader may recall that some time ago indicative planning of the French model was all the rage. A French economist giving a lecture on this subject referred to it as not a *plan indicatif* but a *plan decoratif.* In other words, it had no effect on the actual economy. As part of the planning process, high executives at various companies in the same industry formed committees, which may have given them an opportunity to engage in a certain amount of monopolistic plotting.

While I was at George Mason, we had a student who spoke Norwegian fluently, and we sent him off to Norway to do a doctoral dissertation on the Norwegian economic plan. We thought this would be particularly interesting because Norway has 40 percent of the economy in the foreign trade sector. He discovered that the Norwegian plan was even less effective than the French one. It was indeed printed every year, put out by a small collection of civil servants, but the relationship between it and the world was more or less random. Indeed, he found that in the period he examined, the government did more things that the plans said that they definitely would not do, than things that the plan said that they definitely would do. Perhaps this was merely a coincidence.

Aside from this digression, the main point of this discussion is a certain amount of curiosity as to why organizations bother to build up these plans. Perhaps it has something to do with morale, or perhaps the general spirit of the plan is helpful to the company. It also may be that simply thinking over the whole organization of some company or governmental unit every now and then is a worthwhile exercise, even if the "plans" are not likely to be carried out.

So far we have been talking about ways of adjusting effort to get the maximum control. I would now like to turn to a different way of increasing control: selecting the subjects to be controlled in terms of the ease of control. In a way, this contains a contradiction. An individual who would like to do A thinks A is too difficult and hence does B. It is not really clear that this increases his control. It would depend on his relative evaluation of A and B.

There is a reason to believe that people might be quite happy with the change, however. It is called "reduction of cognitive dissonance". Most people, after a decision has been made, change their preference functions so that their particular decision seems better than it did before they made it. This well-known psychological phenomenon may apply here. It used to be said of General De Gaulle, for example, that instead of doing what he liked, he liked doing what he had to do. Many of us succeed in altering our preference functions so that whatever we find ourselves doing or consuming stands higher in our preference function than it did before we began doing or consuming it. Apparently, this is another example of the widely noted ease with which human beings can be indoctrinated.

But let us now turn to other aspects of selecting what you are doing in terms of what you can control rather than in terms of what basically you would like if control problems did not exist. One example is a particular aspect of government usually brushed over in organizational studies, but which is nevertheless of immense importance and does require an organization: the law. Suppose that we have a dictator who has definite preferences about what he would like to have people do. Among those preferences is a feeling that they should refrain from theft. He announces a law against theft and sets up an enforcement apparatus to prevent theft. Such organizations are fairly easy to design.

There are two different tasks here: one is detecting the thief and the other is making decisions as to what should be done. This last decision includes winnowing out accidental or erroneous detections from genuine detections — in other words, seeing to it that whatever you do about theft, it does not happen too often to innocents who are accidentally caught by the detection apparatus.

The detection apparatus is fairly easy to control; in fact, it is not even necessary to have one. Many societies — the traditional Mohammedan society, for example — did not have any formal government structure to detect thieves. Security depended on individual citizens observing theft of their own property or accidentally finding someone who had committed theft and reporting it to the court system. Probably this detected fewer thieves than would have been detected by a formal police force, but they compensated for that by the ferocity of the punishments imposed. Although this system worked reasonably well, today we object to cutting a thief's hands off.

In countries with formal police departments, however, determining their efficiency in catching thieves is not terribly difficult. You can observe how many thefts occur simply by asking ordinary citizens whether they have had anything stolen recently, and you can observe how many thieves are presented to your court system for trial and what percentage of them the court finds guilty. If the court finds too large a percentage of people innocent, that is, it has standards of proof that make it difficult to convict thieves, then the inefficiency may lie in the court system rather than in the police system. If the punishment allotted for the guilty person is light enough so that, granted how few people are actually caught and convicted, theft becomes a paying profession, then the problem, again, lies with the courts and not the police.

It should be fairly easy for a dictator to determine whether the fault lies with the police or the court system. In the United States at the moment, we have a situation in which the court system is causing a good deal of inefficiency. The courts combine making the punishments light[4] and conviction difficult. It may be true that the dictator is convinced, say, that criminals are mentally ill and in need of treatment rather than punishment and therefore we should not punish them. If so, the whole apparatus may have very little effect on anything. We will assume that our dictator, however, is rather old-fashioned and simply thinks that punishing thieves is a good way of reducing the theft level.

We will consider mainly the courts, not the police department, because the police is an easy area to supervise by the method given above, if we look at their actual detection rate as a percentage of total crimes committed. It should be emphasized here that the court system, in the United States in any event, includes the district attorney and other legal personnel.

In recent years, the federal courts in particular have done a number of things that make it much more difficult to convict criminals. Their strategy has not led to a reduction in the conviction rate because the district attorneys usually only bring cases that they think have a good chance of succeeding. Thus, tightening up the laws of evidence has not lowered the conviction rate which in federal courts is above 90 percent.

As a result of court rules, many people that the police have detected as criminals are null-prossed by the district attorney who feels for one reason or another that the evidence is not sufficient to get through under the present rules. Further, the police may not even arrest people they know are guilty if they anticipate that the courts will free them. This is as much a failure of the court system as the actual acquittals would be, and can be blamed straightforwardly on the judges. The district attorneys and police are simply adjusting to the procedural rules.

Let us stick to the judges only in this apparatus although, as we have pointed out, it is fairly easy to supervise all levels. The judges are *very* easy to control. It is a simple system used by almost every country in the world, although in the United States many of the "judges" are the amateurs that we call jurymen. Let us begin with a professional judiciary of the sort found in most of the world and not the odd rules of the Anglo-Saxon system, and then turn to the jury later.

What is normal is a body of people who make decisions in cases and who are required by law to pay some attention to the evidence. They usually hold a formal hearing of some sort. They should also not have any personal interest in the case. Normally, failure on either of these conditions would be easy to detect, particularly in the case of theft where the judge is unlikely to have any personal interest unless he happens to be related to the defendant.[5]

This simple pair of rules provides a high level of performance of the dictator's laws for punishing theft. The requirement that the judge hold a hearing or in some way become familiar with the case, together with his absence of any motives to do anything except enforce the law,[6] means that he is likely to carry out the instructions. The likelihood can be improved by an appeals system, but let us leave that aside temporarily.

The official who does this kind of work is not necessarily a specialist in the law. Characteristic of most European-type governments, as well as the American system, formal judges are full-time specialists. Of course, the juries that make the decisions in many American cases are amateurs,[7] but this system is not by any means worldwide. In the old Chinese empire, the British empire outside of England,[8] and the Roman empire the judge was simply the principal executive official of the area of concern. The magistrate in China was essentially the central government's control figure in a county, and judging cases was only one of his duties. The same was true of those Roman proconsuls who actually had cases.[9] In the British empire, the district commissioner did everything.

The specialization of judges is obviously not a necessity, and any American who is willing to let his decision go to a jury must agree. What is necessary is that the decision be made by someone who has become reasonably familiar with the facts, and a formal hearing is one way of making certain that is done. But whether the whole thing could be handled by paper — that is, pleadings, transcripts of evidence and so on — we do not know.

The only argument I know in favor of the formal hearing is that the judge and/or jury actually has some contact with the evidence. If they are permitted simply to read things in the quiet of their studies, they may decide not to bother with a good deal of the evidence. Otherwise, the use of written evidence would be much more efficient than oral hearings. The Anglo-Saxon appellate courts operate that way.

The importance of insuring that the decision maker be familiar with the facts in the case explains the almost universal aversion to having "political" intervention in the judicial process. This aversion is found as much in dictatorial regimes as elsewhere, although the dictator himself normally exempts his will from the rule against politics. On the other hand, he rarely has time or interest enough to intervene in most cases. For instance, George Bush might not necessarily be worse at making decisions about a person's guilt or innocence than a jury of 12 randomly selected individuals would, but he actually would probably make the decision on the basis of inadequate knowledge of the facts simply because it is not worth his time to devote much emphasis to the matter.

Therefore, if some dictator were to begin sending orders down to judges on individual cases, it would reduce the efficiency of the court in carrying out his laws. Dictators in practice rarely intervene in individual cases and normally make strong efforts to see to it that their other high officials also do not. Under these circumstances, a dictator's laws can be carried out quite efficiently.

Here, then, is an area where the dictator can get his will carried out with little in the way of supervision. If he wants more supervision than simply depending on the absence of conflict of interest on the part of the individual lower-level decision maker, it can be provided by an appellate court system. After a decision is made by the initial court, it can be appealed to a higher court composed of, say, five judges, possibly even better judges than the regular court, and the precautions we have been describing are somewhat reinforced. The appellate court is even less likely to be directly involved in the case and can be easily prevented from having conflicts of interest. Because it takes a second view of the matter it is probably less likely to make simple mistakes. Again, an easy-to-supervise activity is available for carrying out the dictator's will.

The jury, however, is a special technique. (It is not clear, however, whether it increases or reduces the control which the people of the United States have over the population's behavior by way of law.) The jury itself is an eminently democratic organization in which the 12 people are given an opportunity to get information about a particular case. The laws of evidence mean that they do not get as much evidence as they would perhaps like, but on the basis of the information they receive, they make the ultimate decision. It seems likely that although a sample of 12 is rather small, they tend to reach the decision that the people of the United States would reach if all of them had this information.

On the other hand, there is no doubt that they pay relatively little attention to the law when it deviates from what they think is right. In a way, this is an almost extreme example of short-circuiting. The people of the United States, by way of the jury, are able to obtain what is probably a fairly good implementation of their ideas on law enforcement without any real supervision at all, but there is a tax cost. Periodically, people are compelled to serve on juries.[10]

The problem of the jury and its control raises what is almost the only real difficulty in the use of law as a control mechanism in the way of getting your will done. You have to have an agency that is either indifferent to the actual outcome or tends to agree with you. Historically, most rulers have simply attempted to select judges who are in general accord with the dictator on most matters. Although the jury is an outstanding way of selecting people in general accordance with the average man who is supposed to control in a democracy, the 600-men panels that the Athenians sometimes used would be a better sample of the population.

To repeat, a jury does not mean that the written law will necessarily be carried out if there is some conflict between it and moral principles. Historically, it seems likely that the dictators, kings, and other rulers have tended to select judges who are in agreement with them. In our system the jury rarely pays too much attention to the law. On questionnaires, judges also have been found to give "justice" as either their first or second objective, and to give "adherence to the written law" as, also their first or second objective. Republicans favor adherence to the written law and Democrats favor justice, but both rank the other as second. This is, I think, an expression of the fact that the people giving the orders — the people in the United States, dictators elsewhere — are not absolutely clear in their own mind exactly what it is they want to do.

In the United States when we turn to detailed regulations, and our law has many of them, we normally depend on judges alone and not jury. The regulations are enforced by injunctions rather than by formal trials with a jury, particularly in the case of the income tax in which the Internal Revenue Service is, to put it mildly, extremely reluctant to go before a jury. Only if a wealthy man has done something obvious will they be willing to trust their case to a jury. Otherwise, they have worked out various ways of avoiding the right to a jury trial for the person alleged to have violated the code.

But this particular way of getting your will carried out without much difficulty is obviously only available for a limited set of decisions, albeit important ones. Most governments have depended on this particular technique. Something similar to it exists in private organizations as well. Normally, most companies have an elaborate set of rules for the accounting function which produces the data later used at a higher level for policy decisions. In some cases, this elaborate set of rules is established by the accounting profession itself, but in other cases there are rules for the specific company.

Most companies have an apparatus that enforces these rules in the form of an auditing bureau. This bureau acts much like a European magistrate: it goes out and looks at the subject matter carefully, talks to people, and then decides whether there have been violations. Again, the system works without much supervision because the auditors have substantially no conflicting interests. This is another case in which one's orders can be carried out without much difficulty but, again, only in a limited area.

In both the cases of judges and jury on one hand and auditors on the other, there is one area in which private interests of the decider conflict with those at the head of the organization. The judges may want to take more leisure than the ruler wants, that is to give the cases less consideration than he thinks is desirable. The appellate procedure to some extent deals with this by providing a re-hash of the case with the individual judge possibly being found wrong; hence, his future career is somewhat affected. Of course, if he is an American federal judge and cannot be fired, this variable is not important. Most corporations also have an arrangement under which an outside accountant firm makes an annual audit, and the firm is changed from time to time.

In both of the above cases, it is relatively easy to get exact compliance with the wishes of whoever is making the decisions without a great deal of time devoted to supervision. On the other hand, both cases apply only to a rather restricted area of the possible command structure. It seems likely, however, that the heavy dependence on the law by most states, and the very heavy dependence on accounts by most corporations, are the result of the simplicity of getting orders of the higher-ups carried out in these cases. The purpose of this chapter is to discuss areas in which one can get one's orders carried out easily; hence, the person who wants his will carried out will specialize in such areas.

In one of these cases, auditing, the approach works only if the objective of the man at the top is simply making money. We have pointed out before that people may change their objectives in the direction of what they can obtain. It may be that the dominance of the money-making part of most economies[11] comes from the fact that in this area supervision is relatively easy.

Purchasing is another area where supervision is relatively easy. If one considers companies, the question of whether to make or buy is frequently referred to as a difficult one. One of the major reasons for choosing to buy must surely be that if you have a number of competitive suppliers, your control over what you actually get is probably much easier than if you were dealing with your own manufacturing institution. Indeed there is, as we have mentioned, a whole branch of research initiated by Oliver Williamson pointing out that where a company deals with a monopoly supplier, it may be wise for the company to buy the supplier because of the impossibility of making competitive purchases.

Most people do not think when they purchase something that they are imposing their will on other people, but if you are a fairly large purchaser, it is literally true. Various producers will make efforts to guess what it is you want and provide it for you. They will also make efforts to deceive you a bit as to exactly what they are selling, but that would be true in your own organizational hierarchy as well.

We have mentioned that one way of getting your will carried out is simply to want large profits and use the accounting system as a measure of that. This is a rather extreme example of restricting your desires to something that can be easily controlled; even there, as we have emphasized before, you will not really maximize profits if all you do is pay attention to the accounting system. Still, this is probably the best way of getting your will carried out, even if it requires changing your will.

It is possible that this simple fact is one of the reasons why purchase and sale, manufacturing, and so on, tend to dominate any economy over time. Even the former so-called planned economies of Eastern Europe required such profit-maximizing entities as the Tolkach and the black market to function. The dominance of the profit-maximizing methods is never complete, and economies can be run in which it is quite small. The subsistence agriculture economies in which most people lived until fairly recently comprised such an organization, but in this case, the basic economy was raising food for yourself, and any trade was maximized by using profit-maximizing techniques.

Nevertheless, it is hard to argue that specializing in activities that are easy to control is the be-all and end-all of human society. Fortunately, a reasonably free market using this method of control will in fact achieve many other individual goals, although not everything. Nevertheless, it is an important consideration to keep in mind.

In the previous chapter, we talked about ways of improving your control over areas by simply reducing the area under control. In this chapter, we have discussed increasing your control by attempting to control only subjects that are easy to control. The two ideas are closely related but not identical. Further, the approach of the last chapter did not require any specialization of your own preferences, whereas the ideas of this chapter do. Another characteristic that both have in common is that they assume that you have some way of seeing to it that your inferiors are apt to carry out orders given to them. These incentives and what the lower officials do to prevent themselves from being completely controlled are the topics for the next chapter.

Notes

1. At the time of this writing, the East Germans are revealing what they refer to as luxurious quarters for their higher ups. They are decidedly not luxurious from the standpoint of Westerners. The East Germans' complaint that they were much better than what anyone else in East Germany had, however, is well justified.

2. They have just contributed a wreath to a monument to their victims erected across Dzerinsky Square from the Lubyanka.

3. In the United States, although we do not control in this way, our cost of living index has to be adjusted for quality of the vehicle. For a while, we were using just that particular idiotic measure, the weight of cars, as an evidence of their quality.

4. Mainly by making the prisons expensive and not terribly unpleasant. Indeed, the combination of expensiveness and the not terribly unpleasantness means that the sentences are necessarily short (to save money) and not all that nasty.

5. Courts in which the judges are actually in the pay of criminal groups, as is unfortunately true in certain American cities like New York, are quite unusual in the world as a whole. There is no reason why the dictator, if he actually wants to avoid such activity, cannot prevent it. The bribable judge is a man who of necessity must make his being bribable known to potential defendants. Thus, he must at least to some extent advertise, and it should be possible for the police to detect his advertisement.

6. His motives for that are quite weak, but they are put against zero motives for anything else.

7. So are the assessors who participate in many European trials.

8. This system was not absolutely uniform, but general.

9. In Rome, every effort was made to have the actual cases shoved down to the self-governing municipalities rather than being handled by the government. But those that were handled by the central government were handled by the ordinary officials. As in China, the emperor himself was the ultimate court of appeal.

10. Granted true random jury selection, the tax of compulsory jury service is equivalent to a head tax and thus has a minimum of excess burden.

11. This includes communist economies, although the money-making part of the economy there is frequently either illegal in the form of the black market or concealed in the form of the compensation of the higher officials.

12 INCENTIVES

Most individuals have preferences of their own and do not enjoy carrying out the preferences of others, even if those others are nominally their superiors. The same is true in ordinary commercial transactions. The courteous waiter in a high-quality restaurant probably does not especially care whether the customer gets his order in good condition. He only provides it because that is the way he makes a living, although what is known as pride of workmanship does exist in places.

The waiter is in a particularly clearcut situation. Supervisors in the restaurant see to it that he is reasonably busy and a sizeable part of his income comes from customer tips so that he has a strong financial motive to please them. An individual in a large bureaucracy usually has much greater ability to avoid carrying out the wishes of his superiors if he wants.

The solution to this problem is usually the carrot and the stick. Even slave labor camps make use of the carrot. The reader will recall in the first chapter of *A Day in the Life of Ivan Doneisivich* that the management of the camp asks for volunteers for a particular task rather than simply giving orders. The volunteers are promised a better situation, but Ivan believes it will not be provided and therefore he refuses the opportunity.

165

The use of the carrot and the stick has disadvantages from the standpoint of the people at the top in that there are resources involved which they would like to use for something else. For instance, if you did not have to pay your employees, you could take more vacations on the Riviera. But, unfortunately, you do have to pay them. Indeed, the supervision time we discussed earlier is in part devoted to deciding exactly what rewards would be given to individuals. In our society, we frequently deal with employees of either the federal or local governments, private companies, or nonprofit organizations. There are no actual punishments although this fact is slightly concealed because things are sometimes listed as punishments.

It used to be said that when J. Edgar Hoover did not like an official he would send him off to the FBI offices in Butte. This was regarded as a punishment, but it really was not since the person could freely leave if he wanted. What it was really was reducing his rewards sharply. It is easy to mix up the choice between a cut in the rewards a person receives and in actual punishment. From the standpoint of the person's situation before the change is made, there is no great difference except that it is always possible for the person to refuse to accept the reduction in reward and quit. He cannot do that with a true punishment.

It is one of the characteristics of a capitalist, or, for that matter, any kind of open economy, that the basic method of getting obedience is the carrot — the stick is restricted to preventing crime and things of that nature. A man given a sentence of ten years cannot just decide to quit. One of the characteristics of communism as it was, not as it was claimed to be, was that it depended heavily on the stick rather than the carrot.

Except within the party hierarchy itself and for certain favored intellectuals, there was not really a great deal of legal difference in income available. Furthermore, what difference of income that was available depended upon promotion to executive rank, and only a small part of the personnel in a factory could be promoted to that level. Consequently, only the stick was available. The various arrangements making it hard for the person to quit his job in the Soviet Union meant that, to a considerable extent, the various industries did not compete for labor.

On the other hand, certainly after the death of Stalin and more recently, officials were more reluctant to use the stick. At the time of this writing, the question is open of whether the government of the Soviet Union can change the situation so that the simple stick of firing can be used. Whether they will accept the carrot of differential wages with some of the higher returns going to people who have just been lucky — we have no way of avoiding that — is an open question.

Most American intellectuals prefer the combination of the high productivity that comes from the widespread use of different-sized carrots in a truly free economy with the security that goes with the Russian system. Obviously, the two cannot be combined. The traditional point of view of right-wing U.S. citizens is that incomes should be permitted to vary freely but there should be a safety net into which people can fall. This means, except in criminal matters, a complete dependence on the carrot and not on the stick, but it also means that some very big carrots will be distributed to some people.

Enough of this speculation on life in communism, which now appears to be undergoing a rapid change. Let us turn to the situation of the U.S. official somewhere in the hierarchy, either government or private, and consider the ways in which he attempts to maximize his own preferences rather than the preferences of his superiors. We should keep in mind that some of his preferences probably relate to what tasks are performed by his inferiors. He has a combined problem of obtaining independence for himself and obtaining control of his subordinates. But for now we will discuss the former aspect.

What, then, are the actual desires of an inferior? First, he probably will not want to work as hard as his superior would like him to. He may just not be terribly hard-working or may be hard-working but wants to work on something else. The problem is particularly acute with people who have mental work. It is almost impossible to tell by looking at a man what he is thinking. He may be thinking about the problem which has been assigned to him, or he may not be.

Judgment by result, observing whether he comes up with a solution, is a method, but unfortunately different problems have different degrees of difficulty. A supervisor who is not willing to devote as much time to a problem as the person attempting to solve it, is not really in a good position to tell whether the person has reached the best solution or even whether he has been thinking about the matter continuously over a period of time. By the rather simple procedure of giving a person many problems and then applying the law of large numbers to both the quality and the quantity of solutions, this difficulty can be resolved.

Determining the quality of the solution of these problems, however, is probably impossible unless there is an objective measure. The superior would have to devote so much time to judging these solutions that he would have little time for anything else. Over a very long period of time, by drawing a random sample of a small set of these decisions, the superior could use this method without devoting too much time to it. But we do not know whether this is an efficient procedure.

Physical labor is somewhat easier, but even here, only careful study can determine how much work a person should turn out. The usual method is simply to compare different workers on similar tasks. The foreman has a good idea of how long it should take. In practice, this probably means that strong healthy people do not work as hard as they could and that smaller people who are not in terribly good health are overworked. This discrepancy comes from holding everyone to the same standard. Ways of avoiding this problem do not have general application.

The conclusion we draw from these considerations is that perfect supervision is difficult, particularly with mental labor. Nevertheless, supervisors should try to do as well as they can. In a business firm, increasing the pressure put on inferiors may mean that they quit or that they get paid a higher salary.

We are talking here about the lower-ranking official and his effort to maximize his own utility rather than that of his superiors. Whatever rewards or absence of penalty his superior can inflict or award is part of his utility, although he has others. We have already mentioned his desire normally not to work as hard as his superior would want. Again, this does not necessarily mean that he is lazy. If he is engaged in mental work, he can do idle daydreaming, worry about his personal stock portfolio, or even try to solve a scientific problem of no interest to his employer, all while he appears to be concentrating on his employer's desires.

The federal government has a particularly difficult problem of this sort. Many individual employees have developed strong ideas as to what their particular bureau or suboffice within that bureau should be doing. They may devote much energy to this pursuit rather than the objectives of their superiors. This may be exactly what the government as a whole wants, but more often it is not. Usually it is not something that per se would be contrary to the public interest, although sometimes that can be true as well. But it is normally something that does not contribute, and may well be contrary, to the major drive of the organization as seen by its superiors.

In the Foreign Service, which I left a long time ago, the basic lack of coherence between the desires of the higher officials and the activity of the junior officials was primarily that junior officials were not doing very much. It was not an extremely industrious collection of people, except for individuals who were simply following various special hobbies. For example, one ambassador hated the government head of the country to which he was accredited. This head of government was not on terribly good terms with the U.S. Department of State either, but the ambassador succeeded in being much more negative in his dealings with him than would normally be the case, and his reports back to the United States were also clearly affected by his strong personal feelings.

General Taylor, the commander of the 8th Army during my last few days in the embassy in Korea, was barely interested in what went on in his army and immensely interested in what went on in the Pentagon and in the Executive Office of the President. His efforts relating to his command were geared mostly toward seeing that nothing happened to get him bad reports at those higher levels.

But this method is merely part of the individual's way of dealing with his superiors. If the individual's activity is going to differ from what his superior wants, he must see to it that the information reaching his superior does not indicate any discrepancy. If the individual is carrying out his superior's wishes with perfection, he still wants full control of the information flow because he wants to make sure the good news is passed on.

This discussion of the way a lower-ranking official attempts to control the behavior of his superior by controlling his information repeats things said earlier in the book. The main point of saying it again is that the incentives of necessity are based on information that reaches the superior — information that may be inaccurate either because of random error or, more important, because the inferior wants it to be inaccurate.

The more intense the incentives that the superior puts on the inferior to carry out his wishes, the more the inferior is motivated to distort the information reaching the superior. There used to be a theory of the "band of brothers" in what used to be the British civil service. All promotion was by seniority; hence, there was substantially no reason why any of the people in the band of brothers should deceive any of the others. This does not mean that no such deceit existed. Various informal incentives such as saying nice things or bad things, inviting people to dinner, and so on, depend on the information that other members of the band of brothers have; therefore, there is still a modest need to deceive them on occasion.

To take the other extreme, during the 1930s, Stalin provided what can only be described as extraordinarily severe incentives for obedience to his higher officials. It is likely that this maximized their motives for attempting to control the information he received. Apparently, he dealt with this by killing people for the most trivial information and deviations from his will. Since he was insane, random killing occurred as well.

Let us now turn to incentives themselves and then later mix the information problem and the incentive problem. A strong mythological view exists in our society that positive incentives are better than negative incentives. I think this view is largely motivated by the fact that the former are nicer. Talk about rewarding virtue is more pleasant than talk about punishing vice. The same phenomenon can be seen in modern criminology where most criminologists prefer not to think about punishment as an infliction of pain. They regard it instead an educational process that will rehabilitate. Since we can inflict pain but do not know how to rehabilitate, this attitude is self-frustrating.

The view that negative incentives will not work, especially in complex activities, is contrary to the evidence we have. Solzhenitzyn's *The Second Circle,* which is a novel based firmly on fact, deals with a research laboratory maintained by the Russian secret police and was also a prison for scientists who had done something that irritated the secret police or who perhaps had been picked up in a random sweep. They were incarcerated in this prison and ordered to engage in scientific research. If they refused, they were threatened with various disciplinary measures in the prison, or send to an ordinary concentration camp. So in the novel and in the real world, they conducted the research.

Another example of advanced work obtained by negative incentives, was the German concentration camp at Dachau which contained within it a factory making high tech buzz bombs. In spite of the sole use of negative incentives,[1] prisoners manufactured this hard-to-produce device efficiently and in large volume. Like the research facility maintained by the NKVD, this work was by no means routine. As a result of the American-British bombing offensive, supplies were intermittent and frequently delayed, resulting in occasional rapid changes in the manufacturing process. The prisoners, most of whom hated the Nazis, were compelled by negative incentive to cooperate with these changes.

Negative incentives have been used in many other operations throughout the world's history. Most Southern slave plantations were so. After the liberation of the slaves, the production of cotton and other crops in the South fell sharply because the slaves were not willing to put in the long hours and devoted work in return for a positive reward that they had been willing to put in to avoid a flogging. But this does not mean that the real production of the area fell. The leisure that the slaves could now consume, which they had been prevented from consuming before, clearly was one product of the Southern economy valued by the slaves more highly than they valued the cotton. Thus the net effect was really an increase in the total product. It is just that leisure is not included in the statistics.

*   *   *

It is also a little hard to tell the difference between a positive or a negative incentive. In the last ten years or so the Chinese countryside has undergone a gigantic increase in productivity as a result of an open market system[2] that has permitted the Chinese peasants to obtain positive rewards for their work. If, however, an American farmer were confronted with the range of income and living standard given to the Chinese farmer in return for the same levels of work, the American would no doubt regard it as an extreme example of negative incentives.

Technically, the problem is where the zero point lies that distinguishes positive and negative incentives. Suppose a Southern slave master of the Simon Legree type[3] announces a policy of 50 lashes every Friday for all the slaves, but offers positive rewards such as refraining from whipping or reducing the whipping for those who work hard. We might object that the zero point in the chain should not include the whipping (but there is no intrinsic reason why that is necessary). This is particularly true if we talk about salary levels. Humans are now living at varying salary levels in different parts of the world. What would appear to an Indian peasant as a largely improved income would be regarded as a severe punishment by an American. Indeed, most American prisons offer a higher living standard than is obtained by much of the world's free population.

If the discussion of positive and negative rewards has any meaning at all, it must start from the status quo of the person under consideration. Thus a vice-president of a large corporation who is now being paid $500,000 a year would regard a shift to $250,000 as a severe penalty. Another assistant vice president who is now being paid $250,000 a year would regard a potential increase to $500,000 as positive. Although the change of income is exactly the same for both people, one can only declare the incentive as positive or negative by using status quo as a base, For many people in the company, an income of $250,000 would be regarded as a great positive incentive.

Really severe negative incentives are not permitted in our society. We cannot flog workers, shoot them, or send them to the gulag. Indeed, most of the people who write in this area are academics who have jobs where they cannot be either demoted or fired.[4] Under these circumstances, the negative incentive spectrum is narrow although not zero, and the positive incentive is wide; therefore, it is probably sensible for most people to depend mainly upon the positive incentives. Under these circumstances the sensible thing to do is to set an employee's standard pay lower than you would if you had access to the full range of incentives. Doing so gives you more opportunity to have positive incentives.

Another problem is that positive incentives fairly uniformly cost the supervisor or his employer money, whereas negative incentives tend to be cheap. Indeed, the reduction of the working capacity of the victim of the negative incentive, either through his execution or through his being unable to work hard because he has been injured severely in the course of receiving the negative incentives, are the principal costs of the negative incentive to the employer. In our society, to repeat, they are not permitted. I am certainly not complaining about that fact, but we should keep in mind that the unwillingness to use this kind of incentive system restricts its use, not that it would be ineffective.

Negative incentives do exist in our society, although they are modest. A strong reproach is frequently thought of as a negative incentive, but it is normally mainly important because it carries with it a threat of firing. Aside from firing, things such as imposing fines on employees to be deducted from their salary, lowering their salary or transferring them to a less significant place with lower salary, are all possible but rarely used. Superiors apparently feel that having someone stay around who is unhappy with his position is worse than firing the man and hiring someone else in his place. Because of this attitude, in a flexible labor market such as we have, negative incentives turn heavily in the direction of simply firing.

To repeat, it is not necessarily obvious whether you have negative or positive incentives. For example, consider an auto agency that hires salesmen at a base salary plus commission on sales, with a low base salary. It is difficult to say here whether it is offering positive incentives in the form of commissions on cars or negative incentives in the form of absence of commissions if no sales are made. If the salesmen take the job knowingly, they presumably are willing to accept this incentive system without too much effect on their morale.

If information and control were perfect, it would be sensible to use a large number of small incentives in order to completely control the behavior of the inferior. In practice, we do not have good enough information to do that with most direct employees. Thus we are usually forced to offer bonuses or pay raises or, for that matter, occasionally refrain from making pay cuts over fairly long periods of time considering quite a large bundle of behavior as a unit.

One area in our society where the rewards and punishments are handed out in small increments as a result of detailed specific decisions, however, is when the person making the decision is the residual claimant. Say that the owner-operator of a store gains every time he makes a right decision and loses every time he makes a wrong one. If the decision is an unim-

portant one, his gain or loss is small; hence, he has an incentive to concentrate his attention optimally on big decisions and only give less
attention to small decisions. Although this approach is highly efficient,
the economies of scale and differential individual talents seem to indicate
that it will not work everywhere.

Beginning with economies of scale, consider a large company that is
necessarily large because, say, it is the Ford Motor Company in the early
twenties and is making one-third of the world's automobiles on one assembly line at great savings. In some cases, such companies actually are
owned by a single person or small group, as the Ford Motor Company
was, who gets the optimal incentives. Usually it is a corporation with
wide ownership of the shares. In this case, the residual claimants are the
shareholders, and they do not play a major role in the management.

The solution adopted for this problem in most corporations is to provide a bonus or stock warrant scheme so that higher officials, particularly
the chief executive, find that their income varies according to the fluctuations, first in the profits of the company and second, and even better, the
capital value of its stock.[5] At various times, the income tax law has made
it difficult to offer this kind of bonus, but at the moment bonuses can
be large, as in the famous case of the broker who got $400 million in
one year.

In large corporations, however, although this works for the higher officials, it is difficult to produce a similar system for the lower level — say,
the division managers. The problem is that the divisions are to some extent in conflict with each other, and an incentive system might exasperate
that conflict.

Basically, there are two ways of dealing with this problem, neither of
which is very good, and there are compromises among them. First, when
a friend of mine was working at Ford Motor Company he discovered that
the bonuses distributed to all of the senior employees regardless of where
they worked were simply a function of the total profits of Ford Motor
Company that year. This meant that as far as the bonuses are concerned,
these employees had no reason to undercut each other. They also did not
have much chance of improving their bonus by improving the profits of
their division. They still could consider the possibility of promotion, but
not as much as if the bonus system had been allocated to the individual.

The second case is one in which the accounting division is asked to
compute, insofar as it can, the pure contribution of profit of each profit
center, and then the head of that center is given a bonus based on that
figure. This case embodies the opposite problem. It provides the strongest
possible motives for individuals to attempt to switch profits out of other

divisions into theirs by hard bargaining, noncooperation, and so on. At the same time it also gives them the highest possible motives to work hard and maximize the profits in their division.

Most companies have some compromise between these two systems which gain advantages of each and suffer from the disadvantages.

Another incentive system, and surely the most common in our society, is used by large corporations like Ford for all except the highest ranking officers. It is simply to have the superiors promote and demote and raise and lower salaries according to their views of what the individual contributes to the firm. Formal incentive systems exist because there is no superior at the top level. The stockholders pay little or no attention to the actual management; therefore, an automatic system such as a bonus scheme is certainly better than letting the stockholders vote on who should get what.

Of course, the subjective judgment of the superior is subject to error. If he is given the same bookkeeping data used to compute the bonuses, however, it is likely that his judgment is better than any of the automatic systems I have mentioned. The problem here is giving the person who makes the decision appropriate motives and thus we have switched mostly to such automatic systems.

Profit-making businesses are not the only places where problems of this sort arise. The Pope, as the manager of a very large organization, has problems of who should be a monsignor, who should be bishop, and so on up. In his case, he has some fairly clearcut negative incentives since he can unfrock a priest.[6]

The government is a larger organization, and most modern democratic governments have handicapped themselves by making it impossible for the senior officials to do much in the way of either rewarding or penalizing most of the civil service employees. The people at the top, on the other hand, are rewarded or penalized by the voters who are only somewhat better informed than the average stockholder, and, unlike the average stockholder, do not have optimal incentives from the standpoint of efficiency.

Much evidence now exists on the effect of transferring the operation of various government services from the government civil service to some kind of contract provider who is a profit-making individual or corporation. The savings are usually large, probably because of this defect in the government's supervision process[7] which means that this large cost-saving activity is not taken advantage of as much as one might hope. Furthermore, in many cases the private contractors were able to influence the outcome positively.

In private companies, each individual should ideally receive a bundle of small rewards and penalties depending on exactly how he behaves on the job. An individual entrepreneur has a set of rewards like this, but no one else in the economy does.

The ultimate owner of the business, whether he is a single small man or John D. Rockefeller, may have preferences which are not solely those of maximizing the firm's profit. From the standpoint of the economy as a whole, this consideration is more or less irrelevant. The artist, who instead of producing paintings he thinks will sell well, produces ones that will sell only moderately well but that he likes, is maximizing his own utility even if he is not maximizing the utility of potential purchasers. In a competitive market other people would tend to fill the gap, and, in any event, the entire cost in monetary terms would fall on that entrepreneur.

The same would be true of the owner of a large enterprise. Henry Ford refused for a number of years to replace his Model-T with a more modern and convenient car. This cost him a great deal of money[8] and its main effect on the economy was the growth of General Motors, Chrysler, Nash, and so on. Probably we were somewhat better off with the dominant control of this one monster manufacturer shrinking a bit.

It is in this sense that we can refer to the economic system as optimally efficient, although sometimes we do not want optimal efficiency. As far as I can see, the "industry" that provides cocaine, marijuana, heroin, and other drugs is run by a group of profit-seeking entrepreneurs who are extremely efficient despite the fact that some of their competitive techniques are frowned on by society. Nevertheless, in this case, most people believe that we would be better off if this industry were less efficient.[9]

Many people would say that this industry is inefficient because its customers are injured by its product. This truth can be applied in a lesser extent to many other industries who provide what the customers will pay for, not what some outside observer thinks is the ideal product. If you are the outside observer, too bad. On the other hand, if the outside observer is going to restrict *your* consumption potential, you would object.

In any event, this individual entrepreneur is not what we observe most of the time. For a variety of reasons not well understood, large enterprises seem to work better than small ones in many parts of the economy.

In part, this is simple economies of scale. Perhaps the most simple and famous example is the Alchian and Dempsetz movement of a large crate. Economics of scale encompass more, because a great many large economic enterprises operate different factories in different locations producing different things. These cases probably have economies of some sort in the higher management. Perhaps, for example, high skill in merchandising — which mainly consists of guessing what people will buy — is a rare talent; therefore, it is best used at the head of a large diversified corporation.

I won't argue that this is so. In fact, I do not know exactly why many of these very large organizations such as Fairfield, LTV, and ARA exist. What we can say is that they have won in the competitive fight.[10] In any event, in these large organizations, the incentive problem is real and cries out for a feasible solution, even though it will be far from perfect.

In other organizations, the problem is much more difficult. In the government, for instance, there is no simple measure of efficiency and no group of people who have strong motives for wanting the organization to be efficient (even if like stockholders they have little motive for becoming informed about it).

Here, again, the actual mix of government units is quite disparate. Many different countries comprise the world, and the boundaries of the countries are the result of past wars or, in those cases where there is an irredentist movement, will be determined by the outcome of a future war. These countries have radically different forms of government, running from Castro's Cuba on one end to Switzerland at the other, but within any given country there may be a large number of governments depending on how thoroughly decentralized control is.

This situation is somewhat different from the market situation. There is every reason to believe that a highly competitive market among other things puts pressure on all its participants to achieve optimal scale. Whether this pressure is strong enough and whether simple historical development does not mean that things which were optimal in size and scale ten years ago are still around although there has been a technical change is not clear. What is clear is that very little pressure of this sort exists in the government area.

Traditionally, war has been the main competitive technique for determining size of the nationstates. Unfortunately, war probably does give impetus to states which are the most efficient military machines, but there is no reason to believe they are optimally sized for other functions.

If we look at the mix of local and centralized governments, again, there does not seem to be any significant pressure for efficiency. And, again, history may have led to a division that was efficient at some point in the past and no longer is.

In theory, we have a rather good way of telling the optimal size of government for any particular activity. The smaller the government, down to and including a government that has only one citizen, the more likely it will carry out individual preferences. Suppose a particular government activity can be done either at level A or level B and that roughly half the population favors A and half B. Let us assume that total population is 25, and 13 prefer A and 12 prefer B. Using simple majority voting if they are all in one government unit, 12 people do not get their wishes.

Assume, however, that there are five government units and the 25 voters are divided randomly, 5 to a unit. Although we cannot make exact calculations, it is obvious that the number of people who find themselves in a government following a policy of which they disapprove will be fewer than 12 because 13 voters cannot form a 3-person majority in more than four of the governments. If they do, there will be a fifth government that follows policy B, and where only one person — the one who favors policy A — is disappointed. This gives us nine disappointed people, although with random assortment we would anticipate the system would do better.[11]

This phenomenon — first noted by Pennock — is perfectly general. The more we divide the government up, the fewer the people who will find themselves in a minority. This is true even if there is no voting with the feet; that is, they all stay in a given area. With voting with the feet, the effect is stronger.

This obviously is an argument for smaller governments. Unfortunately, there is an equally strong argument pointing in the opposite direction. Various externalities have different geographic scope. What I do on my property affects what my next-door neighbor can do on his. Furthermore, what we do on our government's territory affects people in other governmental areas. Internalizing these externalities requires larger groups and, in fact, there are externalities large enough so that only a world government would be able to internalize them adequately. Thus there is a strong argument for large governments. It is possible to set these two different tendencies against each other and find the optimal one,[12] thus permitting us to obtain optimal government sizes.

But even this is too simple. We are assuming that the individuals all vote and cast reasonably informed votes — an unlikely assumption, and we are also putting no cost on the time they spend in voting. Addition of these results would no doubt lead to a new optimum that is somewhat different from the one above. Nevertheless, these calculated efficient optimums have nothing to do with the government units that we observe.

History is even more likely to be the dominating characteristic in governmental units than it is in private business. For instance, both California and Nevada are optimally efficient in state sizes. Pretty clearly, it is simply the result of history.

With government incentives, the situation is even worse. I mentioned earlier the civil service which in most Western countries makes it impossible to fire people. In most countries, seniority is important for promotion, with the result that even the reward of promotion for efficiency is limited. The United States has been experimenting with direct monetary rewards administered by higher officials to lower officials, but in my opinion these tend to be routine. It is dangerous for a secretary who has only been in office a few months and who plans on leaving in a few months to allocate these rewards according to what he thinks is the merit of the officials.

Indeed, in the United States, the permanent officials with their security of tenure and their well-established communication channels, especially with the press, may be in a better position to bring pressure to bear on their nominal superior than he is to bring pressure to bear on them. The effect of this on the incentive scheme is obvious.

Nevertheless, the fact that our government is broken up and we are decentralized is clearly an advantage. The Swiss situation in which the decentralization proceeds even further and in which almost any decision by the government can be reversed by popular vote probably provides even better incentives than ours. Certainly their government performs more efficiently than ours.

It is difficult to think of anything one could do about all of this considering that the higher part of the organization, the voters themselves, have no simple easy way of telling whether their objectives are being carried out. In most cases they probably do not know what specific objectives they would like the government to maximize. To repeat what I have said several times, as bad as this system is, the alternative forms of government seem worse.

In that part of the economy where there is strong pressure for efficiency, an approach similar to federalism is one possible solution. The widespread use of franchise operations is clearly an effort to split the entrepreneurial function into two levels.

At the top we have an organization composed of specialists who make decisions in efficient merchandising and other policy matters. At this level, the return in which small policy changes lead to almost immediate effect on the franchising organization is clear. Roy Kroc's building of McDonald's is a famous case.

The organization, however, is made much smaller and less bureaucratic by referring a large number of detailed decisions to individuals who run individual stores, or in some cases small subchains of stores, and whose rewards and penalties are handed out in small quantities depending on how efficient they are because their costs and their returns are both directly personal.

Unfortunately, the franchise system, although it does improve the incentive scheme, is not universally applicable. It is very hard to see how Ford could have run his assembly line by this method, but something can be done experimenting that way. Several industries (I have mentioned building and the New York clothing industry) have many small businessmen engaging in sales and purchases from each other, with the result that complicated items are produced without a centralized organization.

Rumor has it that Chrysler, with the exception of its transmission train, has shed almost all its research in improved technology onto its part suppliers. They buy components, say, brakes, and simply shop around among different possible sellers to get a good quality product, thus putting pressure on the brake manufacturers to do respectable research and to improve design. Whether this is a better method than doing it all yourself, as some other automobile manufacturers do, I do not know. Certainly the Japanese manufacturers have always depended more on specialized suppliers than American companies have.

Here we are back to the kind of puzzle we have dealt with before. Again we find that there is a wide perspective of types of organization and it is hard to say why some companies use one kind and others use another. As we discussed in Chapter 10, one gets the impression that a radical change in structure is frequently more important simply because it is a radical change than because the new structure is an improvement over the old. Perhaps the breaking up of all the little rent-seeking conspiracies is the real function of corporate reorganizations.

Incentives are an all-important tool of management, and the organizational structure is affected by the incentives just as incentives affect the organizational structure. It would be nice if we had better information on these matters than we have, but at least we can make use of what we now know.

Notes

1. Unless you are going to say that permitting you to stay in the camp rather than being killed is a positive incentive.
2. More accurately, an only moderately controlled market system.
3. Simon Legree, of course, was a foreman, not a master.
4. They can be harassed, and in an inflationary period, they can have pay raises denied.

5. As discussed at length in Chapter 10, apparently actual ownership by way of a leveraged buyout is a better incentive.

6. In the past his negative incentives were somewhat more effective.

7. A credible threat to make such a transfer sometimes results in equivalent savings within the bureaucracy itself.

8. He remained a billionaire.

9. As a typical Chicago economist, I am in favor of legalizing these drugs.

10. LTV won its fight for a long time but is having difficulty at the moment.

11. See "Mosquito Abatement," in my *Private Wants, Public Means*, (University Press of America, 1970 pp. 3–28). Also see Yoram Barzel, "Two Propositions on the Optimal Level of Producing Collective Goods," *Public Choice* 6 (Spring 1969), 31–37.

12. It would be necessary here to take into account externalities of one activity on another as well as the pure geographic externalities.

13 SUMMING UP

By now the reader has discovered that I have more puzzles than solutions which could reflect the present level of knowledge in this area. A large group of scholars who got their initial start from the work of Herbert Simon have studied these problems in detail. I usually call them the Williamson group because most of them are organized in a sort of feudal train behind Oliver Williamson. They have discovered a great deal of detailed information.

I have mentioned several times in this book the hypothesis that when two companies are involved in a supplier-supplied relationship and they each have some monopoly or monopsony power over the other, they are likely to merge. I emphasize the word "likely". Many times there is no merger, and other arrangements are made so that neither is able to exploit the other.

Furthermore, even though we can accept the monopsony/monopoly argument, many large corporations involve different divisions that appear unrelated. Most industries have a large collection of companies of different scale and with radically different organizations. For one example, at the time Henry Ford was producing the Model T in a completely integrated way, with Ford iron ore being carried in Ford ships to the Ford steel mill and so on, another prosperous company in England, Singer, was producing a small number of cars per year and was purchasing almost all its components. Both companies flourished in a highly competitive industrial environment.

Other examples can be found in the retailing business, where all sorts of different sized enterprises can be seen with all sorts of different internal structures. Some businesses have pronounced economies of scale, and the total market is small enough so that it is difficult for a large number of different organizations to operate,[1] but this is far from typical. Most companies who do not have government protection suffer from at least some competition. Indeed, the *Journal of Economic Perspectives* offers as a constant that the proportion of manufacturing industries in which the four largest firms accounted for more than 50 percent of output is roughly one-third.[2]

The puzzle of exactly why we have large, highly diversified organizations, other than because of historic development is a difficult one, particularly in the market where there are strong pressures for efficiency. In government, the pressures for efficiency are modest; hence, we would not be surprised to find organizations that are radically inefficient in size.

The best explanation for these large organizations — and one that I offer with considerable caution, partly because it did not originate with me but also because it is not a widely approved position — is that only a relatively few people have specialized talents such that higher executive positions are safely entrusted to them. The first example of this has to do with merchandising skill, whether we are thinking of selling aircraft to major airlines or movies to customers whose average mental age is 14. In both industries, it is important to guess whether the commodity will sell before large sums of money have been spent on design or construction.

It is probably even more important in percentage terms in retailing organizations. After all, they do not spend much on permanent capital compared to, say, an airplane industry which, if it starts work on designing a new transport plane must devote several years and immense amounts of engineering skill to producing just the preliminary model.

Should McDonald's put considerable emphasis on Ronald McDonald? Should they have small playgrounds outside their restaurants? Should they have fixed menus or allow individual preferences for their hamburgers like Burger King does? Apparently such decisions are very difficult and only a few people are highly skilled in making them.

If this is so, then centralization in large organizations that make use of these rare talents — talents that command high returns — is a sensible arrangement. If you can minimize the bureaucratic size of the structure while still centralizing this kind of control through a franchise system, that is also sensible. Most of the monster supermarket chains are, however, centralized from top to bottom. Many of them even manufacture some products on their own.

The rather mysterious talents which, when they are missing as they were in Grant's or in Montgomery Ward, lead to collapse, and when they are present as in Sears Roebuck and J.C. Penny's, lead to great expansion, are probably not only rare but also hard to detect. Perhaps many people are as good or better than the current managers, but there is no way of finding out except to put them at the head of one of these monsters and see how well they do.

Merchandising talent is not the only specialized talent that people at the top require. That rather mysterious entity called administrative ability is also necessary. In many cases, creativity, in the sense of knowledge of what can be done by new technologies and ordering it done, is vital. Most large organizations have elaborate research facilities, but they devote more attention to implementing ideas that come from the sales force or management than to inventing ideas of their own.

All this is an effort to solve a difficult puzzle. What we actually observe is a society of many different sizes of organizations ranging from the individual at one end to the Roman Catholic Church at the other.

Since the time of Adam Smith, it has been part of our culture to make great gains for ourselves by cooperation with our fellow man. Certainly since the Old Stone Age it has been known that we can make great gains for ourselves by competition with our fellow man in a direct and destructive sense. It has also been known since before Adam Smith that competition in a constructive sense is helpful. A partial problem is to get all three aspects into their proper scope and make use of them.

The destructive type of competition we attempt to eliminate by use of police and law. It does not follow that we have succeeded, and indeed the resources put into both police forces and legal activities are considerable in the United States. This cost is borne to prevent a loss, not to make a gain.

When we turn away from the problem of preventing murder, fraud, and theft and face the more constructive part of our activity, we observe again a large number of hierarchical organizations, some big, some small, which react with each other in manners that are partially competitive and partially cooperative.

It is our custom, and one that has been followed in this book, to divide these hierarchies into the governmental hierarchies and the market hierarchies. As a matter of fact, there are many hierarchies that are neither governmental nor market — I just mentioned the Roman Catholic Church — but they have been little discussed here, mainly because I do not understand them.

There is also another immensely important organization in our society, although I do not know whether it should be called a hierarchy. This is the family. Families come in many different forms, from the narrow nuclear family of the Western tradition to the extended family of the East. At least in the United States, families are now undergoing rapid transition. That is the extent of my discussion of them in this book.

In regard to governmental and market hierarchies, I would like to repeat something I have said several times, which is that "sociologically, they are all the same." This does not mean that they are similar in other respects. In the simple market portion of society, most of the people most of the time devote most of their attention to maximizing profit. The accounts are also not a bad way of measuring the degree to which at least some of the inferiors in a large hierarchy are achieving that goal. They are thus subject to continuous pressure for efficiency.

In government hierarchies there is also some pressure for efficiency. Unfortunately, it is not nearly as strong. Indeed, from time to time we set up special committees to look at the government, and they invariably find large inefficiencies. Quite frequently, however, the specific recommendations of these commissions are also inefficient. Nobody has millions of dollars riding on making the best decision. Note here that efficiency has a narrow technical definition. The Gulag seems to have been internally efficient.

On a more prosaic level, it is rare for a company to be in a situation where its profits can be increased by somewhat deceptive advertising or economizing on safety devices or something similar. Here we have a kind of destructive interaction that we would like to have the police and courts prevent. Unfortunately, the police and courts themselves are not very efficient in this area. Furthermore, the police and courts may inflict great cost by preventing the development of new ideas. There has been an immense reduction in the rate in which new and improved medicines are produced. This was caused partly by the U.S. Food and Drug Administration (FDA) which has imposed criteria on new medicine that, first, makes development of new medicine immensely more expensive than it was before and thus reduces potential profits from research; second, it imposes delays on the use of new medicines. Indeed, it seems quite probable that the FDA is right up with Pol Pot in the number of unnecessary deaths it has cost.

The FDA's problem is difficult. Companies are motivated to produce new drugs (leaving aside possible legal damage claims) as quickly as possible, and some of the new drugs will no doubt turn out to be dangerous. On the other hand, the delay in introducing them is dangerous. The FDA has chosen to emphasize the danger of the new drugs and ignore the danger of delay. Hence, it has produced a completely unbalanced scheme which, to repeat, has probably caused many unnecessary deaths.[3]

Another problem has been the development of tort liability for new drugs. This has literally led to bankruptcy for several drug manufacturing companies; others have decided it is just too dangerous to experiment in some areas. A new drug introduced for some disease may, after a considerable period of time, have secondary consequences that were not discoverable at the time it was introduced. Judges and juries have turned out to be extremely generous in damage payments in such cases, and, of course, the drug company is not able to go to the people who are not damaged and collect the value of their benefit from the drug; therefore drugs that are socially desirable may not be produced because of these potential damages.

The point of my digression is that the interaction between different types of agencies, hierarchies, and individuals, is frequently complex. What we want are designs of hierarchies that work well not only internally but also in their interaction with others.

To repeat the philosophy outlined earlier, we have a society in which there are many individuals who can gain a great deal from cooperation and who also gain from predation on others. They can also suffer if they are victims of predation. Furthermore, it is fairly easy to demonstrate that the predator-victim relationship injures the victim more than it benefits the predator. Thus the cooperative relationship is the one we prefer. Its form is various, but we can divide it roughly into two categories: purchase and sale, and hierarchical interrelation. Any good society will have a mix of both categories.

This book has been mainly concerned with the hierarchical structure but I must emphasize that the hierarchies are engaged in market-type interactions that highly influence each other. Some of these hierarchies are governments rather than private companies, and in such cases, the market reaction tends to have much weaker controls. Indeed, such relationships can easily slip into the predator-victim type organization.

With hierarchies, however, there are immense numbers of different organizations in the world. No doubt part of the variance results from history rather than present-day developments, particularly with governmental hierarchies. In the market, however, a hierarchy must be efficient to survive; hence, when we find a number of radically different designs of hierarchy all apparently surviving, we have a puzzle.

This situation is, of course, what we observe in the real world. To repeat an example used earlier, retailing is sometimes carried out by individual stores purchasing through wholesalers, and so on; sometimes by big centralized organizations like Safeway, sometimes by a sort of combination which we call franchising, and sometimes by the kind of thing that is represented by Ace hardware which I have called reverse franchising. Nor is this a complete list of all the different ways these organizations can be set up.

To repeat, the existence of this vast number of different organizations presents a puzzle. The simple solution is that organizational form does not matter very much. If this is true, there are a considerable number of professors in business and public administration who should be encouraged to seek out more constructive activity. On the assumption that it is not true, there is an alternative explanation which is that certain details of the various problems met by these organizations dictate one particular structural form as most efficient. That seems to me the most likely explanation, but as the reader has discovered, I have been unable to put my finger on those detailed reasons.

It is fairly easy to invent a story as to why any particular structure we observe is efficient. I have returned repeatedly to the explanation for General Motors buying Fisher bodies which is the monopoly/monopsony explanation. Certainly, this is a very important part of the explanation; however, we have to explain why General Motors did not buy its principal supplier of frames. The monopoly/monopsony relationship was there, too. Perhaps there is something special about bodies that does not apply to frames, but I cannot say that I have found it.

After our survey of hierarchical forms, we can say a great deal about the way to run them most efficiently. As stated in the last chapter, the use of incentives and well-functioning incentives is important. The basic structure, however, remains a puzzle.

Having frankly confessed that I am puzzled by this, I could put this manuscript in a drawer and hope that in another 20 years of thought I might solve it. Since I am 69, however, that does not seem feasible. The alternative is to present the problem to my readers and hope that they will solve it, preferably in less than 20 years. Ellery Queen mysteries contain a challenge to the reader. I am following that precedent. Can you produce an explanation for these manifold different organizational forms? If you can, you should become both wealthy and famous. You would also confer a great benefit on society. With all of those incentives, surely you will try.

Notes

1. I am personally involved in one that produces a rather specialized but very good cleaning fluid. The particular portion of our company that manufactures this product has four employees and currently fills more than 80 percent of the nation's demand. It is unlikely that anybody will be able to undercut because almost of necessity they would have to start out on an even smaller scale.

2. Julian L. Simon, "Great and Almost Great Magnitudes in Economics," *Journal of Economic Perspectives* 4 (Winter 1990), 149–156, esp. 154. To add a constant of my own, the proportion of manufacturing industries where one firm produces 100 percent of the output is roughly zero.

3. See Peltzman, Sam, Review of *Innovation in the Pharmaceutical Industry* (by David Schwartzman) in *Journal of Economic Literature*, 16, 149–50. Also Wardell, William M., "Economic or Medical Criteria, or Both, in Policy Decisions about Medicines?" in *Journal of Health Economics*, 2, 3, 275–279, 1983.

INDEX